The Tibetan Art of Parenting

The
Tibetan Art
of
Parenting

From Before Conception Through Early Childhood

Anne Hubbell Maiden and Edie Farwell

Wisdom Publications • Boston

WISDOM PUBLICATIONS
199 ELM STREET
SOMERVILLE, MASSACHUSETTS 02144

Library of Congress Cataloging-in-Publication Data

Maiden, Anne Hubbell.
  The Tibetan art of parenting : from before conception through early
childhood / Anne Hubbell Maiden and Edie Farwell.
    p.   cm.
  Includes bibliographical references and index.
  ISBN 0-86171-129-7 (alk. paper)
  1. Birth customs—China—Tibet. 2. Pregnancy—China—Tibet.
3. Childbirth—China—Tibet. 4. Infants—Care—China—Tibet.
5. Parenting—China—Tibet. 6. Tibet (China)—Religious life and customs.
7. Tibet (China)—Social life and customs. I. Farwell, Edie. II. Title.
GT2465.C6M35 1997
392.1'2'09515—dc21   97–17055

ISBN 0-86171-129-7

02 01 00 99 98
 6   5   4   3   2

Photo Credits
Cover photo, pp. 42, 64: © Thomas L. Kelly; p. xxii, back cover (bottom): © Susan Lirakis
Nicolay; title page, pp. 92, 112, 130, 156, back cover (top and middle): © Janet Ryan
Richardson; pp. 12, 24: © Amina Tirana

Illustration p. 20 © Andrew Weber

Book design by: Adie Russell

Wisdom Publications' books are printed on acid-free paper and meet the guidelines for the
permanence and durability of the Committee on Production Guidelines for
Book Longevity of the Council on Library Resources.

Printed in the United States of America.

I dedicate this book to my children,
Benjamin Nansen Hubbell and
Lisa Hubbell Mackinney,
to my grandchild,
Hannah Mackinney,
and to Dugu Choegyal Rinpoche
and the Tibetan people.

Anne Hubbell Maiden

I dedicate this book to my parents,
Jean and Frank Farwell,
who gave me the best childhood imaginable,
and to my husband, Jay Mead,
for the joy of birthing and raising
our children together.

Edie Farwell

Contents

Foreword

I am delighted to provide the foreword for this work on Tibetan parenting, a subject that has rarely been discussed outside of the Tibetan community until now. While on the one hand our approach to bringing new lives into this world derives from valuable traditional wisdom, on the other hand, our customs also contain perhaps undesirable ancient superstitions. For instance, many Tibetans believe that a baby should not be taken outdoors until it is a certain age, and even then that imaginary evil spirits must be warded off by smudging soot on the child's nose. These are uniquely Tibetan cultural beliefs and are certainly not recommended to other societies.

Despite these superstitions, we Tibetans also possess valuable traditions surrounding the wonderful experience of childbirth to share with the world community. In an era when people around the globe are exchanging ideas and benefiting from the knowledge of others, I feel that this title is timely and that it will be extremely helpful to many parents.

One of the traditions that I value most is based upon our Buddhist belief that achieving a human rebirth is the most precious accomplishment of all because only humans have the power of reason, and therefore the potential to liberate themselves from worldly suffering. So, for a Tibetan woman who chooses to become a mother, bringing a precious new human being into this world is the most wonderful and challenging responsibility of her entire life. In this respect, I also appreciate the supportive roles that the whole community plays in giving special attention to both the mother-to-be and to the child, right from conception through adulthood.

Another aspect of traditional Tibetan motherhood that I admire is that while not neglecting medical practicalities, traditional Tibetan women faced childbirth in a very natural way. I feel that while we are fortunate to have access to the latest scientific discoveries, we should also approach pregnancy and childbirth in a holistic, healthy way and avoid becoming dependent on medication and other interventions.

In one way, it is sad that Tibetan women are deprived of their homeland and scattered all over the world today. But when we consider this from another angle, it is very fortunate that we have joined voices with the world community of women and can now share our wisdom with others.

Rinchen Khando Choegyal
Minister of Education, Tibetan Government in Exile
Director, Tibetan Nuns Project, Dharamsala, India

A Note from the Authors

From Anne Maiden

In keeping with Tibetan birth ways, as I was to discover, this book began with a dream. "It is time for the world to know about Tibetan birth" resounded in my ears one morning as I traveled from dream to waking consciousness. My inner response to this message was a combination of certainty, willingness, and curiosity. My trust in dreams had grown through decades as a psychotherapist. And for years I had journeyed at every opportunity to study birth in cultures around the world. My passion was kindled by an inner need to heal my own experience of American hospital birth in 1960. Practices from other cultures, I believed, could enrich options for families, birth attendants, and Western medicine. What was the next step to learn about what the world ought to know about Tibetan birth?

Three days later the mail brought an announcement of a study seminar on cultures, to take place in the Himalayas, sponsored by the California Institute of Integral Studies. The seminar site was a fifteen-minute walk from the Tibetan refugee community of Tashi Jong in Himachal Pradesh in northernmost India. One of the faculty members was Joanna Macy, who had known the spiritual leader of the community for twenty-five years. Since I already knew Joanna and other faculty members, it was now clear how I would meet Tibetans, the first step to learn and share their ways of birth.

There were seven months to prepare before we departed. Tibetans, scholars, and translators told me there was little documentation about Tibetan birth, only a few sentences in two books: *The Tibetan Book of the*

Dead and *Death, Intermediate State and Rebirth.*[1] So, having sought out and read these resources, I kept on asking and seeking. And at last I found a Tibetan doctor in San Francisco, Lobsang Rapgay, who told me there was a great deal to be known about Tibetan birth traditions. Over the next few months, he brought me books, answered my questions, translated texts from Tibetan to English, gave me a letter of introduction to a librarian relative in Dharamsala, and, much later, took me to visit his elderly mother, who had been a midwife in Tibet.

In India, before the seminar began, Joanna introduced me to Dugu Choegyal Rinpoche, from the neighboring Tibetan community. His training, based on the teachings of his spiritual lineage about preparation for birth, had begun at age thirteen, before he left Tibet. He had taken on a major spiritual responsibility from his teachers—to teach others—and he asked Joanna for her help in this work. From that moment, there was no doubt about why I had come. Choegyal Rinpoche's first words set a context for all our meetings: "Birth comes from beginningless time and boundless space."

Over the next weeks I shared early morning meditation instruction, seminars, meals, pilgrimages, walks to Tashi Jong, and long talks with other participants in our seminar. One was then an anthropology graduate student named Edie Farwell (degree completed in 1990), who had developed a strong interest in Tibetan culture and planned to stay longer in the Himalayas. Her probing curiosity and vivacious focus on the lives of Tibetans drew my attention. I had already decided to engage an assistant for my research on birth customs. Walking and talking, we noticed mutual commitments, and it became clear that a book on Tibetan ways of birth was taking shape. So began twenty months of near-daily focused work together, and seven more years of collaboration to fulfill the initiating dream and to bring this book to the world.[2]

As I write, my first granddaughter is gestating in her mother's womb, and I look forward to remembrance and use of these gems from Tibetan wisdom through all the phases of our relationship.

From Edie Farwell

I had several motivations for co-writing *The Tibetan Art of Parenting*. I wanted to collect and document a body of knowledge that was in danger of being lost as Tibetans fled their homeland after the Chinese invasion. I also wanted to analyze how a refugee population keeps its beliefs and customs intact despite geographic dispersal and the threat of cultural extinction.

It seemed to me that the Tibetan communities in exile preserved their cultural identity remarkably well despite the many pressures resulting from the occupation of their country. I wondered if the Tibetans could serve as a model for other refugee populations, and if I could discover some clues to their success. Given the Tibetan Buddhist belief in reincarnation and the passing of knowledge from one lifetime to another, I suspected that childbirth and the rearing of children played a pivotal role in the preservation of knowledge and the continuity of cultural identity.

I also wanted to compile a resource of Tibetan birth customs that would be useful and accessible to both Tibetans and non-Tibetans. By researching, analyzing, and documenting this universal event from the perspective of a culture very different from my own, I hoped to determine more clearly which aspects of the birth process cross cultures, and which are culture-specific.

Another reason for my interest in this project was my desire to integrate my long-standing interest in Tibetan Buddhism with my own experience. Since my first visit to the Himalayas at the age of nineteen I have felt a deep attraction for Tibetan people, culture, and history, and a great respect for Buddhist philosophy. At the time we started work on this book I was just beginning to plan for my own first baby, and I felt that an exploration of Tibetan birth wisdom might greatly enrich my own conception and birth process—which indeed it did.

The Tibetan emphasis on the integration of the mental, emotional, spiritual and physical provided a holistic framework in which to balance the various parts of my life to allow sufficient room for a baby. Drawing from ideas generated while working on this book, I prepared to conceive, give birth, and rear a baby consciously and deliberately. For example, my husband and I created our own conception ritual that, for us, marked our readiness to bring a child into this world. This approach gave us not only a richer and fuller engagement with the birth process than I might have experienced otherwise, but continues to enrich our interaction with our child's ongoing development as well.

Whether or not to bring a child into this world, in which overpopulation and overconsumption are significant threats to the continued well-being of our planet, is a weighty decision. I found that the spiritual philosophy and natural wisdom of this ancient culture helped me to purposefully and thoughtfully prepare for the responsibility of giving birth, and continues to inspire me to provide as healthy an environment as I can for our children. I hope this book will help others as well to provide a framework for conscious conception, healthy birthing, and nurturing of well-loved babies.

A Note on Perspective

The rest of this book is written, for the sake of clarity, from a first-person perspective. The book reflects the experiences, research, and insights of both authors. Both authors lived and researched in Dharamsala and other Tibetan communities in India, and each worked with and interviewed Tibetans and Tibetan scholars and teachers in the United States. Both authors researched the available written material on Tibetan childbirth. So "I" in the following chapters represents the feelings, observations, and reflections of both authors.

The characters in the book are also composites. Except for a few named scholars and friends easily recognizable as themselves, the characters are fictional. They are based on a number of Tibetans each author knew and talked with, and they represent the diversity of families and lifestyles found in Tibetan refugee culture in northern India in 1989. Using composite characters provides a rich representation of the types of families with whom the authors were in most contact and allows protection for the privacy of these families. Except for a few instances in which a Tibetan served as translator, the interviews were conducted in English, one of the official languages of India. Tibetans also assisted by providing translations of Tibetan texts.

As in any country, traditions and customs in Tibet vary from region to region, from family to family, and from individual to individual. Likewise, in exile, Tibetan customs vary from refugee community to refugee community. An aim of this book is to represent these differences, while at the same time describing an overarching Tibetan approach to childbirth that both encompasses the varieties of customs and articulates traditions that are distinctively Tibetan of which there is still knowledge in Tibetan refugee communities.

Preface

The Purpose of this Book

A primary purpose of this book is to introduce Western readers to an integrated view of birth, represented by the Tibetan culture, in which the physical, emotional, mental, spiritual, relational, and environmental elements of birth form one whole—a respected, unbroken continuum of life and interconnected experience. Closely related is the purpose of preserving the wisdom of an ancient people. This book aims to document Tibetan birth wisdom and practices for future generations of Tibetans who may not have the fortune to grow up in their homeland; and for Westerners, so that they may learn from and expand upon their knowledge and understanding of childbirth.

This preface places Tibetan ways of birth, very briefly, into the larger context of other cultures' approaches to birth, with an intention to make the contribution of Tibetan views more vivid for all those concerned with birth and childcare. A Tibetan way of seeing is endangered both by cultural repression and relocation, and by modern biomedical and technological dominance over the natural process of birth in family and community. Among many indigenous peoples, the meaning of medicine is to create harmony among sacred realms, the earth, and all life on earth. To practice medicine is to use one's sacred power to do good for the benefit of all.[3] A further purpose of this book is to stimulate a synthesis of modern and traditional approaches to medicine. This book is intended to serve as a bridge between Eastern and Western cultures, and to further the exchange of childbirth knowledge and cross-cultural appreciation and understanding. Drawing from the learnings of many cultures, the advantages of appropriate biomedical advances could become an integral option within the framework of a low-cost, low-tech, family-centered, culturally and environmentally compassionate approach to birthcare.

Parents are the most important influence in choosing birth practices which connect—rather than separate—families, children, and inner knowing. However, whether we are parents, pediatricians, psychologists, midwives, obstetricians, nurses, family physicians, childbirth educators, social workers, marriage and family counselors, students, sociologists, medical researchers, public health policy planners, legislators, or anthropologists, a knowledge of Tibetan practices can inspire us to create the conditions in which health, family, community, environment, and spirit are at one in a continuum of birthcare. This book intends to help parents of all backgrounds honor and learn from the Tibetan people; to select from Tibetan ways those that will enrich and enliven their own birth preparations and care for children; to help preserve a part of Tibetan culture; and to stimulate compassion, wisdom, and participation in the creation of birth options everywhere.

Childbirth is a universal and timeless event, with extraordinary impact on our well-being. It serves us well to learn as much as we can from cultural traditions, as well as innovations, in order to create and choose for ourselves the most beneficial ways to give birth.

Organization and Sequence of the Book

This book is organized around an expanded view of the birth process, as a series of seven stages, beginning before conception and moving through early childhood. The seven stages are preconception, conception, gestation, birth, bonding, infancy, and early childhood. Each of these seven stages is part of a continuity in care, valued across cultures, which contributes to healthy birth and life for child, mother, and family. Accordingly, a chapter is dedicated to each stage.

1. Preconception

Before conception, family and cultural beliefs and practices influence the physical, social, and spiritual environment in which a couple conceive.

2. Conception

   Beliefs surrounding conception and how it occurs, as well as accepted practices, tell much about the values of a people.

3. Gestation

   Care during gestation (from the growing baby's point of view) and pregnancy (as experienced by the mother and her community) tells more about understanding and preparation for birth.

4. Birthing

   The events closely surrounding birth, from the onset of labor through the emergence of the newborn, cutting the umbilical cord, and handling the birth of the placenta give an intimate view of family and community relationships and the value accorded each individual.

5. Bonding

   Bonding provides the basis for ongoing relationships and occurs across all seven stages.

6. Infancy

   In the stage of infancy, both parents and their offspring undergo rapid physical, psychological, and social change in new relationships to both family and culture.

7. Early Childhood

   Early childhood marks the phase in which a child may tell us about birth and prebirth experiences and begins to form conscious intentions about becoming a parent.

The seventh stage brings us full circle to the stage of preconception. What occurs in all these stages influences the health and nature of the child to be born, as well as generations to come.

Treasures of Tibetan Birth Wisdom

Toward the completion of my inquiry—after reviewing notes, transcribing tapes, studying further sources, interviewing more Tibetan scholars and parents, writing, contemplating the knowledge that Gyatso (an honored lama) and my other friends had shared with me, and then writing some more—various insights from the Tibetan heritage surrounding birth and childcare began to emerge. As you read this book, these insights will become familiar as their applications are explored and illustrated from one chapter to the next, through each of the seven stages of birth. In order to facilitate this familiarity, the insights will appear at the beginning of each chapter, from preconception through early childhood. Since these insights are a precious treasure of Tibetan culture, they are referred to as "gems" of Tibetan birth wisdom.

The reader will find that each chapter has its own emphases. Through stories, medical information, and family and religious traditions, the book gathers and reflects the wisdom Tibetan culture has to offer as we choose and act in our lives to care for the beginnings of life. A medical researcher, for instance, may discover hypotheses, or an anthropologist find insight into an unexamined cultural ritual, while parents may remember a practice they want to bring into their family ways.

After Gyatso read my list of gems of Tibetan birth wisdom, he commented, "Only when an analytical approach is integrated with meditative contemplation do we know what is true, for truth is what we know in our experience of deep consciousness. So each of these insights, gathered as they are from observation and study of Tibetan heritage, can be useful in your life only as it resonates with your own innate wisdom." As Gyatso urges, the reader can take from each section what is useful now in his or her life, holding the integrated Tibetan view, which embraces physical, emotional, mental, spiritual, relational, and environmental aspects of birth in its wholeness.

For my part, I suggest that you use Gyatso's guidance to test each "gem" with your own knowing. If it "speaks to your condition," as the Quakers say, then it is likely to be useful in your life.

Tibetan mother with baby twins and toddler on a roof in Dharamsala, India.

Prologue: Beginnings

The world has become communicably smaller today, and with respect to its limitations, no nation can survive in isolation. It is in our own interest to create a world of love, justice and equality, for without a sense of universal responsibility based on morality, our existence and survival are at a perilous precipice. The qualities required to create such a world must be inculcated right from the beginning, when the child is young. We cannot expect our generation or the new generation to make the change without this basic foundation. If there is any hope, it is in the future.

—*His Holiness the Fourteenth Dalai Lama of Tibet*[4]

The Chinese Occupation of Tibet in 1950

For centuries, Tibetans, living on the roof of the world, were long isolated from others by the natural barrier of the great Himalayas. The few foreigners who did visit Tibet wrote of being impressed by the stark beauty of the land, and the vitality, joy, humor, and profound spiritual life of the people.

In 1959, however, the Chinese government imposed martial law on Tibet, finalizing an invasion begun in 1950, and imposed the burden of military occupation on the country. The 1960 Geneva Report of the International Commission of Jurists concluded that "acts of genocide had been committed in Tibet in an attempt to destroy the Tibetans as a religious group." Four decades later, the environmental, social, and cultural changes wrought by the Chinese government and military have been devastating to Tibet's ancient and sophisticated civilization. All but a dozen of

1

six thousand monasteries and their irreplaceable books and religious relics have been destroyed. Over a million Tibetans (out of a population of six million) have been killed since the invasion, and roughly seven million Chinese have been relocated into Tibet. Consequently, there are now more Chinese than Tibetans in Tibet, and twice as many people altogether, trying to live in a delicate ecosystem.[5]

The land itself is as much in danger of destruction as the Tibetan culture. Vast Tibetan forests have been clear-cut. Once-abundant wildlife has disappeared due to the fact that in Tibet, as in China, the Chinese military regularly shoot animals on sight. A few years ago, a young Tibetan suggested a project to reforest some of the extensive acreage the Chinese government has logged. He was jailed for two and a half years.

The ancient culture of Tibet is now severely endangered, and it has become difficult, if not impossible, for Tibetans to practice their traditional ways, including medical and birth practices. A complicating factor of the birth process in Chinese-occupied Tibet is that many women, and even young girls, are forced to undergo sterilization procedures. Many have been sterilized before they have given birth at all. Repercussions of these sterilizations are seen in India and Nepal as mothers flee Tibet, bringing their daughters to relatives or orphanages in the hopes that they will have a safer life than they would in Tibet. The Tibetan orphanages and schools in India also report an increase of pregnant women who are leaving Tibet to give birth in India or Nepal, then leaving behind their babies to go back to care for other children and family members still in Tibet. The fact that pregnant women are choosing to make long, arduous trips, climbing over high Himalayan passes, rather than give birth at home, suggests that presently the life of a pregnant woman or a newborn child in Tibet is risky, at best.

Many Tibetans and others feel that the Chinese government is trying to eradicate as many Tibetans as possible so there will be more room for Chinese people in Tibet. Already, indigenous Tibetans, who have lived for centuries in harmony with the land, are outnumbered by the seven million or so Chinese citizens who have been moved into Tibet. The fact that Tibetans are facing not only the loss of their culture but this genocide makes it even more important for Tibetans in exile to record and uphold their traditional culture.

Present-day Tibetan Culture

Amidst all this oppression, the prevailing Buddhist tenet is to practice compassion toward oneself and others at all times, including grave hardship. Consequently, while many Tibetan Buddhists have become refugees, dispersed and scattered from their homeland like the sudden splashes of wildflowers found in the high Tibetan plateaus, they have chosen to share their cultural beliefs and practices with others, as so many families did with me.

His Holiness the Fourteenth Dalai Lama, the spiritual and temporal leader of Tibet, emphasizes that it is not the Chinese people who have harmed Tibet. Indeed, many Chinese, especially minorities, have suffered equally under their government's policies. It is the actions of the Chinese government and military that the Dalai Lama and other Tibetans speak out against, not the Chinese people or culture. The Dalai Lama stresses compassion toward the Chinese people who have also suffered, and even more compassion toward those Chinese who have inflicted suffering on others. This enlightened view has won the Dalai Lama tremendous respect worldwide as a peacemaker.

There is now also global recognition of the compassion and wisdom Tibetans have to offer the world. Evidence of the world's appreciation for Tibet's unique culture and philosophy can be seen in the award of the 1989 Nobel Peace Prize to His Holiness the Dalai Lama and in the celebration in 1991 of the International Year of Tibet.

The current Chinese government has made many parts of Tibet largely inaccessible to foreigners and has heavily restricted and controlled cultural and medical research, so I traveled to the northern Indian town of Dharamsala, where many Tibetans live, to pursue my study of Tibetan ways of birth. It is there that the Indian government kindly made available a cottage and land to the Dalai Lama after he escaped across the Himalayas in 1959. Seeking to preserve Tibetan culture, the Dalai Lama set about establishing a Tibetan community in exile until Tibet was free for Tibetans to return home. That wait has already lasted over forty years. Now that a full generation of Tibetans has been born and raised away from their homeland, it has become even more imperative to document traditional Tibetan customs and culture so that its natural wisdom remains accessible to young Tibetans and others.

Over the years, the upper part of Dharamsala has become the heart of Tibetan culture outside Tibet. In Dharamsala, the Dalai Lama has created a Tibetan government in exile, including a constitution, his five-point plan for peace, and his proposal that Tibet become an international environmental preserve.[6] He and others have also constructed the Tibetan Medical Institute, the Library of Tibetan Works and Archives, the Tibetan Children's Village, and other institutions necessary for the preservation of Tibetan culture and religion. These institutions and the people associated with them have been invaluable resources to me. They maintain a continuity of Tibetan culture that has been suppressed in parts of Tibet itself. In Dharamsala, the traditional family culture has survived, along with much of Tibetan birth wisdom.

In addition to Tibetan and Indian cultures, Dharamsala has an international flavor; its population includes foreigners drawn to visit, live, or study among the Tibetans there. The visitors may come as students of Tibetan Buddhism or as curious travelers attracted to the many Tibetans who have a knack for finding satisfaction and even joy amidst life's varying circumstances, despite the tragedies caused by the invasion of their country.

Many believe this ability comes from the Tibetan Buddhist religion, from cultural influences, or from living high atop the world in the Himalayas. The Dalai Lama, one of the most truly free-spirited and joyful people I have ever met, comments in his book *My Tibet*, that, "Tibetans are naturally a happy and well-adjusted people, thus forming a distinct society. These are qualities praised and regarded as worthy of emulation by sensible people the world over." I wanted to discover the ways in which these characteristics enter the Tibetan birth process and what specific customs might enhance, or hinder, their transmission.

Present-day Tibetan birth practices are derived from a rich collection of medical knowledge. The integration of the physical and spiritual elements of health—what we now call the "mind-body connection"—has been practiced in Tibet for centuries. From the third century on, Tibetan leaders held forums that included healers and scholars from surrounding countries, and there is evidence to indicate that Tibetans were the first people to study and illustrate conception and development of the fetus through the thirty-nine weeks of gestation.[7] Tibetan medical practitioners culled from the Chinese, Indian, and Arabic-Greek traditions what they believed would work best for them, given their environment, lifestyles, and native constitutions.

Tibetan medicine used in birthcare is drawn from these culturally diverse sources. The available treatments include pulse diagnosis, acupuncture and moxibustion, extensive use of specially prepared combinations of herbs and spices, related timing of medications, diet, urinalysis, visualization, mantra, meditation, prayer, sounds, sand painting of *mandalas*, barley-flour sculpture, and a sophisticated system for pacifying chaotic mental and spiritual forces within one. And in all these treatments, including those for birth, the relationship between doctor and patient is held sacred.

The Families

In telling the story of Tibetan birth practice, to make accessible this vast treasury of information, I have woven together stories of my interactions with three extended families. I grew particularly close to these three families, spending countless pleasant days visiting their homes, schools, libraries, health centers, monasteries, nunneries, and temples for special ceremonies, rituals, and events. I talked with them about preparation for birth, the birthing itself, and care for infants and young children. Each family offered me a different perspective on Tibetan birth, having had different experiences and influences in their lives.

Dorje and Lhamo

The first family I met included Dorje and Lhamo, a friendly, active couple in their late twenties, and their two sons, Tenzin and Gyamo, aged four and two. All were born in Dharamsala after each of their families had left Tibet in 1959 to follow the Dalai Lama into exile. Their lifetime in an international town has meant that they have assimilated elements of other cultures into their lives. Lhamo was pregnant when I first met her and was very much hoping for a daughter this time. Although Lhamo and Dorje have chosen to bring up their children as Tibetans, they have integrated ideas from both Western and Indian cultures into their traditional cultural beliefs. They are thoughtful and articulate about differences between living as Tibetans in India and what their lives might have been like in Tibet. They also notice, and are interested in, the influences that their contacts with Westerners and Indians have on their lifestyle. Being Tibetan is a basic identity which they and others in Dharamsala strengthen through teaching visitors about Tibetan ways.

Like most Tibetans, Dorje and Lhamo are Buddhist. They adhere to the main teachings and perform the fundamental rituals and ceremonies—although they give less time to the rituals than their parents did, a trend for most Tibetans in exile in Dharamsala.

Lhamo and Dorje live in a small, comfortable house in the middle of town, and are actively involved with their many friends and neighbors, as well as daily town life. Both are professionals. Dorje studied Tibetan medicine at the Tibetan Medical Institute in Dharamsala, completing the five year training, and is now a doctor of Tibetan medicine at the local clinic. Lhamo helps dispense prescriptions and keeps the books at the clinic. Lhamo and Dorje both enjoy being in touch with all the patients and passers-by who stop at the clinic each day.

Lhamo and Dorje share their home with Dorje's mother, Yeshe, who was a nurse in Tibet and now helps out at the clinic and with her grandchildren. I also got to know Dorje's sister, Paldon, who teaches at one of the local schools; and I met their brother, Dhonden, and his wife Lhakpa Dolkar at their niece's welcoming ceremony.

Palmo and Ngawang

The second family with whom I spent much of my time was Palmo and Ngawang, their three children, and their lama uncle Gyatso. Palmo and Ngawang are in their late thirties and have lived near Dharamsala for nearly nine years, since leaving Tibet. They retain a strong emphasis on Tibetan traditions in their daily living, though they also include what they have learned since they came to India. Their two boys are ages five and nine, and their daughter is thirteen. They had another child, who died when she was three. When she was a toddler, times in Tibet had been particularly severe, as there was not much food available with the influx of Chinese. She was too small and weak to withstand the malnutrition and hardship.

Ngawang runs the only shop in their small village, about two miles around the mountain from Dharamsala, selling fresh produce and staples such as barley, lentils, rice, flour, candles, and other items the villagers regularly need. Most of Ngawang's customers are Tibetans, although every now and then an Indian will buy something. Consequently, he remains immersed in Tibetan culture. After work he usually goes home to be with his family and visit with neighbors. He participates in public activities in town on special occasions, such as Losar, the Tibetan New Year.

Palmo spends most of her day at home, tending the house and children and knitting sweaters, which she sells to a store owner in Dharamsala. Palmo, too, was pregnant at our first meeting, and she later gave birth at home to a healthy baby boy before I left Dharamsala. It was an easy birth—though they had been worried at the time, as the year before Palmo had given birth to a boy who died during the delivery. This calamity made Palmo extra cautious during her pregnancy, as well as in her care for their newborn.

While Palmo and Ngawang don't interact much with Indians and Westerners, they are friendly and open if someone should make the effort to know them. I made the trip to their village often and came to feel very close to both of them and their family, including their uncle, Lama Gyatso, with whom I had many long talks.

Tashi and Tsering

The third family I got to know well was the most traditional. Tashi and Tsering, in their middle thirties, had recently come to Dharamsala from Tibet. A major reason for their exodus, although they much prefer their homeland, was that Tsering was pregnant and they didn't want to have the baby in Tibet with the current difficulties. They were not able to bring much with them and had to depend on their relatives in Dharamsala for financial support and help getting established in their new home. Since they hold fairly traditional beliefs, they have needed to adjust to the fact that some Tibetans in India do not practice or observe the customs they thought everyone took for granted as true and necessary. At the same time, however, they are pleased to find and become a part of such a thriving Tibetan community.

Tashi and Tsering have five children: three girls, aged thirteen, seven, and two, and two boys, aged eleven and four. The children help take care of one another and assist their parents as they get established in their new life. Two other children died a couple of years ago in Tibet—the eldest son and a daughter who would have been nine. Tashi's parents, Rinchen Lhamo and Lodro Zangpo, came with them from Tibet and are making a gradual adaptation to Dharamsala. Traditional Tibetan Buddhists, they feel a profound sorrow that they are not able to spend their last years at peace in their own land.

Tashi is a skilled *tanka* painter and Buddhist scholar, having spent fifteen years of his early life studying in a monastery before rejoining his family to help with the crops. A couple of years after leaving the monastery, he married Tsering and they started their family. Tashi is unable to establish himself yet as a tanka painter in Dharamsala, so he has taken a job at the Tibetan Library assisting other tanka painters. He has little time to study or read the old texts that he loves, but his friends at work are good to him and he is content for the time being.

Tsering takes care of the children and Tashi's parents, and sometimes helps cut vegetables for a friend's restaurant. She is good at making the most out of what they have and has created a warm and loving home for her family, despite financial difficulties. Tashi's mother, Rinchen Lhamo, was a midwife in Tibet, and was generous in sharing information with me. She assists with local births when she is invited.

Further Connections

Visits with these three families extended to various siblings, children, aunts, uncles, and grandparents, whom I also got to know and talk with.

And visits with these friends led to interviews with a mix of people who were interested in or involved with childbirth. Some were people who worked at Delek Hospital, the local Tibetan hospital for Western medicine, others were midwives or doctors, nuns, *rinpoches* (reincarnated, highly realized beings), teachers, librarians, scholars, students, shopkeepers, government officials, and members of families who were having, or recently had, babies themselves. Insights and personal experiences shared by all these generous people form one cornerstone for this compilation of Tibetan birth customs, practices, and beliefs. The second cornerstone consists of interviews with Tibetans and Tibetan scholars now in the United States and other countries. The third involves an extensive review of Tibetan literature and teachings related to birth from before conception through early childhood. The fourth cornerstone is the ongoing inspiration of a courageous people whose culture is in danger of becoming extinct.

I had heard from a number of sources that childbirth is not readily talked about in Tibetan culture. Therefore I was somewhat surprised, and also delighted, that men and women were so open with me and generous with their knowledge. I came to find that this openness was more often the case than not. Though childbirth is seen as a private matter, almost everyone I talked to was more than willing to tell me their views. Often they suggested aspects of the subject for me to research. Even monks were direct and forthcoming, though it is well-known that monks seldom talk about such things with women.

Perhaps people felt freed from social constraints to interact with me because I was an outsider. Or they may have wanted to help a visitor. Perhaps part of the willingness to talk about childbirth was due to a universally shared feeling throughout most Tibetan communities that their culture is in danger of being lost and any attempt to record it is valuable. In any case, people entered into discussion and explorations with an openness that defied the customary reticence about such subjects.

The Sanctity of Life

The Tibetan perspective provides a refreshing and inclusive integration of the physical, emotional, mental, and spiritual aspects of birth. Such a view emphasizes the unity and wholeness of a birthing mother and family, rather than attributing to each of them separate roles and services. Family members work and plan together in every part of the birth process, from family planning before pregnancy through care in early childhood. Recitation of prayers and repetition of mantras are as crucial in each stage of pregnancy as dietary and medical concerns.

This practice stems from the rich spiritual life of the Tibetan people. The sanctity of all life is valued, respected, and passed along in Tibetan cultures. A Tibetan friend once told me, "Life is a continuation of other lives, and is part of an intricately woven web of relationships. The creation of a life is not an isolated event, but is a manifestation of a series of inter-related lives and beings." Tibetan culture is based on a continuity of life after life, as well as a thorough integration of all aspects of life.

In the Tibetan view, birth is part of a continuum within which each individual life has its full cycle of physical and spiritual development, of growth through relationships with others, and of connection with the environment. "Birth comes from beginningless time and from boundless space," one lama told me.

In the Dalai Lama's words, "Our belief in reincarnation is one example of our concern for the future. If you think that you will be reborn, you are likely to say to yourself, I have to preserve such and such because my future incarnation will be able to continue with these things...the idea of reincarnation gives you reason to have a direct concern about this planet and future generations." To elaborate, "Everything depends on one's own karma. This means that one's life situation in the present depends on one's actions and motivations in the past and that one's future is thus capable of being molded through one's actions and motivations in the present."8

The quality of each life, whether it be human, animal, or even a fly, affects all future life. In the same way, the birth process, from before conception, through conception, gestation, birthing, bonding, infancy, and early childhood, affects each child's health and inner peace in growing into man or woman and on throughout life.

The Dalai Lama once remarked about a photograph of a Tibetan man, "His face represents the Tibetan people, with an expression that shows gentleness and sincerity, plus an attitude that is not discouraged or depressed."[9] The ability to pass these traits on to future generations, regardless of what Tibet's future may be, is a crucial part of preserving the integrity of the culture. The birth of children signals hope for the future of the Tibetan people, who work for the continuation of the sacred life inherent in their culture.[10]

Tibetan women tossing tsampa during a wedding ceremony.

1: Preconception

Gems of Tibetan Wisdom Before Conception

◊   *Preconception is a time for preparing body, emotions, mind, and spirit to invite a child into the womb and family.*

◊   *To prepare for conception, couples may reassess their life plans and change physical habits to cleanse their bodies of toxins and nourish themselves with healthy food; they may also consult an astrologer about their compatibility.*

◊   *Spiritual practices—including special prayers and mantras, prostrations, pilgrimages, rituals, and blessings from a lama—are also purifying preparations for conception.*

◊   *Communication with the spirit of the child to be conceived may occur through dreams, inner knowing, a bodily sense, or a special feeling.*

◊   *Parental choices before conception attract the child who will incarnate, and so influence the nature and quality of the child who enters a family.*

Beginnings

In the Tibetan tradition, birth practices begin long before the actual birth, even before pregnancy. Tibetans give significant weight to each of the seven stages, the full continuum from preconception through early childhood, not only to the birth itself, as is so often the case in the United States. During the time before conception, or preconception, couples prepare themselves in many ways. It is an important time to prepare body, emotions, mind, and spirit so that all is in readiness to invite a child into the womb.

Most people realize that during pregnancy emotions and sensations are heightened; Tibetans believe that these same feelings can occur in the period before conception. Some people have a strong feeling of anticipation about conception. Others may sense the spirit of their child or have particular dreams, as well as experience special concerns for physical and spiritual care. When a woman or man feels an inner readiness to conceive a child, their thoughts and choices before conception can have special meaning and power. Many will focus more awareness on what they are doing with their lives and bodies. Couples may reconsider plans and change physical habits to clear their bodies of toxins. They may eat healthier, more nourishing foods. They may pray or recite mantras more often, or with greater intensity, in anticipation of nurturing new life.

At the same time, while many Tibetan people consider the birth process a profound and religious experience, there's also a fundamental sense that it happens naturally, like eating and breathing. Conceiving and giving birth to a baby are normal experiences for millions of women, and preparation can be almost unconscious.

Of the mothers I interviewed in Dharamsala, Lhamo (who, as mentioned earlier, is married to Dorje, is the mother of two boys, and works in the Tibetan medical clinic) represented a more significant Western influence in her lifestyle and outlook. Nonetheless, she expressed intuitive feelings in referring to the time before conception. "With my first son," she said, "I somehow knew a baby would be coming soon. We had recently married and we both wanted children, so I was prepared in a vague way. But there was another feeling, as if my body were preparing itself for us to conceive a baby. Unconsciously, my mind and emotions cooperated."

In a spiritual sense, the conception and birth of a baby is part of the long view of continuing lives and rebirths. So preconception includes the time when a woman is getting ready—emotionally, mentally, spiritually, and physically—to receive a new being into her womb, a "precious human life" as Buddhists would say. Consciously or unconsciously, her body and psyche can feel, at a deep level, that conception is imminent.

Marriage

In the Tibetan tradition, marriage is generally viewed as the first step toward having children. In a culture like Tibet's, in which most families have children, a wedding is considered to be the beginning of a public commitment for children to come—the potential for pregnancy. When a couple marries, they lay the groundwork for conception and are often unconsciously preparing for children. And when couples consciously prepare for conception, that groundwork is intensified. The energy gathered through thoughtful preparations for conception, it is believed, may attract a consciousness seeking rebirth.

Tibetans don't have blood tests or other formalities at the time of their marriage. Instead, almost every couple has their stars done. The astrologer studies the stars of the man's and the woman's births, to see if there are any conflicts, or any indications of difficulty in conceiving children or with the relationship. If they want to marry and their stars don't match, they seek a remedy. Special prayers are considered beneficial. At this time, couples may also plan how many children they will have and when, and prepare themselves for conception. Most, however, make few plans and take the pregnancies as they occur.

In the Tibetan view, one's conduct before conception attracts the being who will choose to incarnate through a mother and father, and so directly influences the nature of the child who will come into a family. While it would be difficult to prove this hypothesis through research, it's not too far-fetched to extrapolate that parents who prepare themselves for conception, both consciously and unconsciously, are more likely to give birth to alert, content, and peaceful babies.

Family Planning

In general, Tibetan men and women marry (except for those who join a monastery or nunnery) either through family arrangements or by their own choosing, and fairly soon thereafter start a family. Traditionally, a woman could have two or more husbands, usually brothers, or, less often, and mostly among the wealthy, a man could have two or more wives, usually sisters. These customs still exist in parts of Tibet, as well as in some of the refugee communities when they support the survival of a family group. When a woman has more than one husband, her children usually consider the eldest husband to be the father.

Both Tibetan medical and spiritual texts describe how a married couple can plan the conception of their children. However, in general, few Tibetan couples, other than dedicated spiritual practitioners, take part in active family planning. While most people are aware of options for contraception and fertility, an overwhelming belief in the naturalness of conception flows through the relationship of wife and husband. Most couples seem quite comfortable about being pregnant and feel it is an accepted outcome of sexual intimacy. And in every marriage the whole extended family prays for children, as human birth is considered to be rare and precious.

Even though a Tibetan couple may not be planning a particular pregnancy, they generally start to prepare for conception on many levels, laying a path for a child to join them. New parents around the world describe with awe the profound feelings that the birth of their first child aroused in them. Even those who do not believe that they need to prepare for conception often find themselves involved in new behaviors. They may choose to eat healthier foods, get regular exercise, or clear up any nagging illnesses. They feel that they want their bodies to be at their best. People in many countries and traditions believe that there is a spiritual element in childbirth, beyond the biological event. Tibetan birth traditions have demonstrated this belief for centuries, promoting psychological and spiritual preparation. As holds true for all Tibetan ways, purifying body, speech, and mind are intrinsically intertwined.

In contrast, while many American couples give consideration to preparing for the birth process, their preparation often begins with family planning: the decision to have children and the best time to start a family. People often begin by examining *if* and *why* they should have children, and even when this decision has been made, they only have children when they are ready to provide a good home for them. Couples may plan carefully, put money aside, and decide when the best time would be. There are practical reasons to do this: children are expensive, more women work outside the home, and many parents feel it is better to provide a good life for a few children than a meager one for many.

For a number of reasons, including an increasing Western influence, many Tibetans have begun to follow this practice as well. In general, Tibetan families used to believe that the more children in a family the better, and many expatriated Tibetans feel that they should have as many children as possible to help their culture survive. But in Dharamsala and other refugee Tibetan communities this attitude is changing. Everyday necessities are expensive, especially the cost of schooling. Consequently, many people are planning more carefully and are having fewer children than they would have had in Tibet. And as couples have access to a wider range of contraceptives, they are able to control the size of their families.

Dr. Lobsang Dolma, a woman doctor who practiced medicine in Tibet, made great innovations in Tibetan medicine, including a more open approach to birth issues and contraception. She opened a clinic in Dharamsala where she gave free treatment to anyone in need and gave many lectures on Tibetan medicine, which her students have compiled and published.[11]

Dr. Lobsang Dolma

Dr. Dolma's story illustrates the extraordinary endurance and determination of many Tibetans to preserve their culture. The following account was published in the U.S. magazine *Women of Power*:

Dr. Dolma was not, of course, the first woman healer in Tibet. Women have always been healers there and she is the thirteenth in an unbroken line. Her father was chief physician in a free healing center in western Tibet. Lobsang was chosen to be his successor when she was fourteen. The Chinese invaded Tibet just as she began her practice. Her father died of torture during interrogation and she became head of the hospital at age twenty-five. As one of the most skilled and educated people in her district, she was a prime target for re-education and, a year after the invasion, she became aware that the Chinese had made concrete plans to remove her to Peking. One night she packed a bag of medicines, tied her two young daughters to her back, and left. Traveling with only the light of the moon and stars, sleeping in caves during the day, she evaded the Chinese sentries and crossed the Himalayas into Nepal. In India she worked on an Indian road building project. Later, after setting up a practice, she was appointed chief physician to the Dalai Lama's medical center, a position she held until 1978.[12]

Dr. Dolma died in 1985, but the clinic that she established in Dharamsala operates to the present day. The daughters she carried across the Himalayas have carried on this tradition of medical care since her death: her eldest daughter continues to carry on her mother's work and runs the clinic in Dharamsala. Dr. Dolma's younger daughter runs a clinic in Delhi.

In her clinic, Dr. Dolma made and passed on a traditional method of birth control for planning families, consisting of nine to ten different kinds of pills made from herbal, animal, and mineral extracts compounded together. Some of the pills are designed to control conception for a few months, some for a year, some for even longer periods, and some, the medical texts claim, permanently. For many—Indians, Tibetans, and Westerners—her pills were effective; for others they were not.

Younger Tibetans in communities in India also use Western forms of birth control, such as the diaphragm and spermicidal jelly. In the religious texts there are also sections on rituals and spiritual practices to facilitate birth control, as well as conception.

Spiritual Preparation

In Tibetan communities it is the job of the lamas, the spiritual advisors and teachers, to facilitate the connections between people and their deities in personal and family matters. In exchange for their spiritual guidance and protection, Tibetan people help support lamas with offerings of food and money. Consequently, as a natural part of the spiritual preparation during preconception, most couples, though sometimes just the woman, will go to a lama to get his advice and blessing. They may even specify the preferred sex of the child (if they have three sons, for example, they may wish for a daughter). The lama then prescribes appropriate rituals or prayers to specific deities. These ceremonies are then performed to enhance the fulfillment of the couple's wishes.

For example, a Green Tara ceremony is commonly performed for those who wish to conceive. Green Tara is the meditational deity of compassionate action. She is often portrayed as sitting in a lotuslike position, as are many Buddhist deities, but with her right foot extended as a symbol of stepping out into the world. One can find many statues of the vibrant Green Tara goddess, holding a lotus flower to her left breast symbolizing power and purity. Her right foot stretches down, signifying readiness to step into action, while her left foot is usually folded in the contemplative position. The two together symbolize the integration of wisdom and action. Her right hand is typically stretched out on her knee with the palm up in a gesture of giving. Tara is revered as the miraculous savior who rescues all beings from suffering. She is also regarded as the mother of all buddhas, and as such is considered especially responsive to those preparing to conceive.[13]

A couple's meditation on Green Tara could involve chanting praises to Green Tara, detailed visualization, and identification with and strengthening of her qualities of wisdom and compassionate action within themselves. It is also common for parents to ask a nunnery or monastery in the area to conduct some of the rituals that lamas suggest for conception. Tibetans have highly evolved rituals and traditions and have incorporated intricate and exacting rituals into their spiritual practice over the centuries. Their use of ritual is somewhat like a science, very precise and expectant of specific results for specific acts. Prayers and rituals are performed by monks or nuns to appease the deities and entreat them to give the couple a child. Tara is often turned to in the case of an urgent request, when there's a need for immediate help. During the rituals, nuns or monks will recite the entire Green Tara ceremony—chanting, ringing bells, clashing cymbals, drumming, and all the while directing Tara's energy to the couple who have asked for special blessings and to the baby they hope to conceive.

ༀ་ཏུ་རེ་ཏུ་ཏྟ་རེ་ཏུ་རེ་སྭཱ་ཧཱ།

Illustration of Green Tara and Green Tara Mantra.

Purification

In preparation for conception, it is common to purify oneself by seeking release from the consequences of any harm done to living beings. In Tibetan Buddhism, negative karma comes through any action motivated by greed, ill will, or ignorance. For instance, desire, hatred, jealousy, or other vengeful thoughts would contribute to negative karma, as would killing or harming sentient beings, including insects and animals. Fortunately, the effects of actions committed in past lives as well as the present one may be cleansed or purified.

There are many paths to purification, including the recitation of specific prayers, the performance of ceremonies, and pilgrimage to holy places. The foundation for all these practices is the act of going for refuge in the Buddha, the Dharma, and the Sangha. By reciting the refuge formula, which has its own rhythm and melody, Tibetans bring themselves into the protective presence of their teacher, the Buddha, the Buddhist teachings or Dharma, and the Buddhist spiritual community, or Sangha.

Prostration, a traditional gesture of homage and an antidote to conceit, when coupled with a heartfelt sense of regret, is a powerful method of purification in Tibetan Buddhist culture. Prostrations are often done as part of the preparation of cleansing oneself for conception. Prostrations, performed by both men and women, can be done in two ways: in the simple manner of a short or abbreviated bow, in which one touches one's forehead and knees to the ground, or in the full body-length prostration. In the full prostration, the hands are pressed together, raised first to the top of the head, then to the chin, down to the chest, and then the person stretches full length on the ground with their hands and arms stretched beyond their head as their forehead touches the ground. During the entire exercise, mantras are repeated and are combined with specific visualizations. This is a physically rigorous exercise.

Circumambulation is another common form of purification. One walks clockwise around a *stupa*, monastery, or temple while saying prayers or repeating mantras, such as the six-syllable mantra of Avalokitesvara (the Buddha of compassion, Chenrezig in Tibetan), OM MANI PADME HUM. This is the best-known Tibetan Buddhist mantra and can be literally translated as "Hail to the jewel of the lotus." Its purpose is to activate the energy of compassion in one's consciousness, or mindstream. The number of mantra recitations is usually counted on one's *mala*, or prayer beads, like a rosary. One way to accumulate merit, a measure of virtue or "good deeds," is through the action of circumambulation and by uttering the mantra. In the Tibetan view of karma, in which one's every action will eventually bring about its effects, actions of merit counteract or neutralize actions of wrongdoing, harm, or thoughtlessness, and so may purify past misdeeds or mistakes. Whether in prostration, in circumambulation, or in reciting the six-syllable sacred mantra, mindfulness and the number of repetitions is important. Tibetans try to do their personal minimum every day, counting on their malas.

This sort of rigorous spiritual and physical preparation for conception is not uncommon; Tibetan Buddhists customarily make pilgrimages, pray, visit lamas, and work to purify themselves when they wish for something, such as a child. Buddhism teaches that everyone has the potential to achieve enlightenment, so Tibetans naturally believe that everyone can work to purify themselves. Through this purification, Tibetan Buddhists believe that they can develop a more direct connection to the spiritual— including spirits in the *bardo* (in between) state waiting to be reborn.

Tibetan couple receiving ceremonial scarves during their wedding.

2: Conception

Gems of Tibetan Wisdom for Conception

◊ *Life is ongoing, and the spirit seeking incarnation is attracted by the specific energetic quality of the parents, even as they engage in intercourse.*

◊ *The environment at conception is important; it is recommended that a couple meditate on love, compassion, consciousness, or gentleness and avoid anger, attachment, jealousy, aggression, or fantasies.*

◊ *Merit and karma, as well as healthy sperm and ovum, determine which of countless sentient minds seeking incarnation will be conceived in the womb of the mother.*

◊ *The time of conception may be known by a feeling of extraordinary bliss or by dreams, and may be assisted by planning intercourse at the time of greatest fertility.*

◊ *At the time of conception there is a great spiritual opening; 72,000 energetic channels are activated in both mother and father.*

◊ *Tibetan medicine includes nine or ten different herbal, animal, and mineral pills to control conception for different periods of time: some are effective for a few months, some for a year, some permanently.*

◊ *Infertility may occur as a result of dysfunctions of the energetic system through congenital causes, psychological causes, or karmic causes; each has its own treatments in Tibetan medicine.*

◊ *Once conceived, the developing fetus forgets its earlier life experiences until later in gestation because the shift involved in the transition is so profound.*

Genesis

Conception, the generative meeting of the egg and the sperm, ignites their unification to generate the process of growing a new baby. In Tibetan literature, the ova is called the "red seed of the mother" and the sperm the "white seed of the father." For the majority of Tibetans, like most people, the exact moment of conception may not be explicitly known. Often, it is only after a woman discovers she is pregnant that she will estimate when the actual conception took place. For some, though, a special feeling comes and a couple knows the moment they have conceived.

Dr. Lobsang Dolma spoke about this time in her *Lectures on Tibetan Medicine*. She said that often a couple will feel more bliss than usual, thereby knowing they have conceived. Others may plan to conceive at a certain time. They may watch their cycle carefully so that they know just when they are most fertile and plan to conceive then.

In Tibetan legend, human creation came about quite differently. In Lati Rinbochay and Jeffrey Hopkins' translation of *Death, Intermediate State and Rebirth*, a text from the eighteenth century, the description of the creation of the first human babies gives perspective on the evolution of birth as we now know it.[14] According to Tibetan legend, the first humans had seven features: spontaneous birth, an immeasurable life span, all sense faculties, a body pervaded by its own light, major and minor marks of a buddha, sustenance by the food of joy without eating coarse food, and the ability to magically fly in the sky.

All this changed, however, when humans began to eat coarse food. Then, the legend continues, the unrefined part of the food turned into feces and urine, and the male and female organs protruded as openings for elimination. At this time a male and female who lay together connected these organs, and a sentient being formed in the womb. These are the steps through which birth from a human womb evolved, so goes the story.

Between Death and Rebirth: The Bardo State

The Buddhist view of birth is spacious. It encompasses vast cycles of death, bardo (the state between death and rebirth), and rebirth. The experience of bardo is a result of the life experiences and actions, or karma, of the being who enters it. It can be quite frightening or seductively pleasant. In the final phase of bardo a being enters the realm into which they will be reborn. Beings with a high degree of spiritual development often choose the place and family into which they will be born. Their choices are made in order to help other beings gain liberation from the suffering of cyclic existence (the endless round of death and rebirth).[15]

In Tibetan Buddhism, the overall goal is to attain enlightenment, or liberation from suffering, for the sake of all sentient beings. In this perspective, the continuity of a being's work is facilitated through reincarnation. A bodhisattva is one who strives for enlightenment to be of the greatest benefit to sentient beings. "Human birth is so precious," Gyatso once commented, "because in this life we can accumulate enough merit to attain buddhahood and be able to work for the removal of the sufferings of all sentient beings."

To illustrate this perception of life, one can imagine a circle similar to the "recycled" logo, except that it has two gates: one is birth, the other is death. Life as we know it follows the opening of birth; what Tibetan Buddhists call bardo follows the opening of death. So one who has recently died is in the bardo with the major task of searching for the right conditions for the next rebirth.[16]

In the traditional view of the bardo state, the intermediate being has many capabilities which most Westerners would regard as psychic abilities; these include aspects of omniscience, the ability to be at different places at one time, and the ability to move through various spaces such as doors and solid objects. While in the intermediate state, this invisible consciousness has sense faculties and a kind of subtle physical form that has similarities to a physical body.

When the being is about to be reborn, it wanders, looking for the right habitat. A being actually sees various couples having intercourse and is karmically attracted to specific parents by their special energetic qualities. So depending on the predominant quality—love, lust, tenderness, violence, drunkenness, or the like—the being will be drawn to a particular couple according to their energetic state.

Dr. Lobsang Rapgay is a Buddhist monk and scholar trained in

Tibetan medicine and Western psychology. His expertise in both disciplines is apparent when he describes the Tibetan view of what happens during conception. "In Tibetan culture, when an intermediate being comes into a body, it experiences various sensations, depending on karma, and the effects of actions committed in past lives. If a being has good karma it is an incredibly pleasant experience, like going into a beautiful house and hearing peaceful and pleasant sounds. If one's karma is not so good, it is unpleasant: one hears lots of clamorous noises and experiences uncomfortable sensations and foul smells. One may have a sense of entering a marsh, a dark forest, a small hole in the ground, or a dark cave from which there is no escape. The sensations depend on one's own state during conception, the qualities of the parents, and one's karma."

Dr. Rapgay indicates that when the child, or the wandering consciousness, enters the womb, the trauma of coming into physical existence represses the memory of all past experiences. With conception, the child forgets for a time its last life, earlier experiences, and previous traumas. Later, during gestation and at birth, consciousness comes alive again. The environment of the womb, resulting from choices the mother makes, also influences the consciousness of the embryo.

Though most Tibetan parents are not consciously thinking of the journey through the bardo when they are conceiving a child, they accept the existence of intermediate states and recognize that bardo is a very important phase of being. In one of our interviews, Lhamo asserted that when she was at Bodh Gaya (in India), the sacred place where the Buddha attained enlightenment and where she had gone on a pilgrimage to purify herself for conception, she became aware of many intermediate beings who had died and were now looking for a place to be reborn. "My friend said I should pray and ask for a special baby. But I didn't ask for any baby in particular. I felt that many people had died for different reasons and that whoever is praying to be born again in a better life could come and be born through me. So she is the lucky one," Lhamo joked, patting her large belly.

Lhamo believed her coming daughter, or son, had some karma with her to have been the one to be conceived in her womb. "Everything in the birth process is linked with karma," Lhamo continued. "The mother, the father, and the baby are all connected by karma. There are so many millions of beings who die daily and want to come back. If they have a chance to become human, they surround every man and woman who are together. Thousands surround us. But only the one who has karma to come to us gets in."

Lhamo said she had been trying to conceive for over a year and felt that she did not become pregnant earlier either because she and her husband were not fully prepared or the time was not yet right. However, she felt that in the two weeks she had devoted to purifying herself at Bodh Gaya, she had prepared, both physically and spiritually, to conceive and receive one particular human consciousness, who was waiting in the bardo state.

The Process of Conception

A few developments during conception are covered in exquisite detail in *The Tibetan Book of the Dead*, a compelling and essential Tibetan text that provides a guide to the successive states and experiences that the bardo being may have after death and before rebirth. The successful navigation of these experiences may lead to profound spiritual insights, fortunate rebirths, or even liberation from the cycle of death and rebirth. Death is an integral part of birth in Tibetan Buddhism. Rebirth as a human can take place only after the death of the intermediate or bardo being is complete.

Among the teachings are specific descriptions of transitions in the intermediate state. When one is coming back toward the material universe, various steps take place on the way to rebirth. The clear light consciousness which occurs at the death of the bardo being begins, in the inner vision of the being, to transform. The inner vision of clear light gives way to one of complete darkness, then one of radiant orange-red light, then one of brilliant white light. As consciousness continues to progress toward a material level, the inner visions are likened to a sputtering candle about to go out, then a vision similar to sparks in smoke, or fireflies, then a smoky vision, and lastly a mirage-like vision. In the next instant the consciousness joins the egg-sperm complex at the moment of conception. The teachings indicate that there is a great deal of spiritual activity at the time of conception, and 72,000 energetic channels in both the mother and father are powerfully activated.[17]

In *The Tibetan Book of the Dead,* instructions are given for choosing and entering a womb. The bardo being is told to concentrate on "a family where the father and mother have faith; and taking a body with merits which can benefit all sentient beings;" it should then affirm, "I will do good." The recommendation is also made to "call on the name of the three jewels, and take refuge in them," referring to the Buddha, the Dharma, and the Sangha.[18] As ether gives way progressively to earth and the sense perceptions return to a bardo being, the material body comes back. From having briefly perceived a sense of unity after death, the experience of separation is reestablished as the elements of the ego begin to form.

According to the text, the bardo experience is followed by rebirth as a human being only if you are extremely fortunate. A Tibetan saying compares the chances of being reborn as a human to the chances of a blind turtle putting its head through a golden ring floating on the surface of the ocean when the turtle surfaces, which it does about every five hundred years. Tibetans see human life as a rare and precious opportunity to increase our own wisdom and compassion, to help others, and to use time wisely.

It has been said that conception, birth, and, death are the most important events of our lives. The traditional Tibetan description of conception uses evocative and lyrical words and images to depict the conditions for conception as well as the physical event. In many ways, the traditional explanation is very much like a story, the tale of "How does a human life begin?" This story combines the physical and spiritual elements of conception. The relationship between male and female energies is considered to be vital. Tibetan teachings describe how sexual energy is related both to the material and nonmaterial universes and subtly brings the two together.

As mentioned earlier, according to Tibetan tradition, a human being is conceived through sexual intercourse when the red seed of the mother is mingled with the white seed of the father, and the two are mixed with the very subtle mind and wind, which is essentially the consciousness of a being. Dr. Dolma describes wind as "a strong force that we cannot see, but one that has a crucial function." She likens it to blowing on a fire so that it becomes stronger. "We blow the fire with bellows and we cannot see the air, but still the fire grows."

Conditions for Conception

Tibetan tradition notes that there are many physical and spiritual conditions that need to be met for conception to take place. It is when all of these aspects are balanced in a person that he or she is most likely to conceive a physically and spiritually healthy baby. Virtually every person interviewed stressed the importance of integrating mental, emotional, spiritual, and physical aspects of a person—for general good health, and especially for conception.

The special conditions for conception are described in detail in Tibetan texts. It is written that after the final dissolution in the process of death, the being is free to be conceived in a mother's womb and thus to start the birth process anew. In order for an intermediate being to be reborn in a mother's womb, three favorable conditions must be present and three unfavorable ones must be absent.

The three favorable conditions are the following. First, the mother must be free from disease during the time following menstruation. (According to *The Ambrosia Heart Tantra*, conception may occur for fertile women between the ages of approximately twelve and fifty, for three days each month, when the winds open the door of a woman's womb.)[19] Second, the intermediate being must be nearby and wish to enter. Third, the male and female must be attracted to each other and have intercourse.

There are also three unfavorable conditions to be avoided. First, the womb must not be obstructed by wind, bile, or phlegm, which have their origins in desire, aversion, and ignorance, respectively.[20] Second, neither mother nor father may have faulty seed, which is to say, conception will take place only when the semen and the ova descend together and both are pure. Third, the intermediate being must not have karma that interferes with or fails to attract its birth to that particular male and female. They in turn need to have accumulated the karma to become its father and mother. Once conception has occurred, the red and white seed are mixed in the mother's womb. They create what is called the regenerative fluid, which causes the formation of the fetus in the womb.

Dr. Yeshe Dhonden, a well-known Tibetan doctor who was formerly chief physician for the Dalai Lama, currently runs a medical clinic in Dharamsala and travels the world meeting with medical students and seeing patients from many nationalities.[21] Dr. Dhonden describes similar criteria for conception and the successful formation of the fetus, five in all. The first requirement is the sperm, and the second, of course, the ova. Third is the consciousness of a being wandering in the bardo whose time is ripe for rebirth. Fourth is the conglomeration of the five elements—earth, fire, water, air, and space. And fifth is the karmic relationship between the being seeking rebirth and the parents.

The sperm and the ova must have healthy qualities that support the formation of the fetus. It is said that the qualities for the sperm are whiteness, heaviness, sweetness, and frothiness. The ova should possess a red color, like that of hare's blood, it is said, and the ability to leave no fast stains on clothes. If they don't have these qualities, then the sperm or the ova is defective and the coitus is sterile.

Traditionally, there are three ways for the regenerative fluid, sperm, and ova, to reach the mother's womb. The intermediate being can come in through the man's mouth, the top of the male's head, or through the vagina of the woman. Those who have reached high spiritual attainment may choose their next conception, enter the father's mouth and go down through his sexual organ to the mother's womb. To such a one it seems that they are entering a palace or mounting a throne. As stated earlier, it is believed that as the intermediate being dies and moves toward rebirth, it experiences a series of visions from clear light to mirage. In the center of the semen and blood mixture—which has descended from the 72,000 spiritual channels—it connects to its new "birth-state." Mental imprints from actions in previous lives arise. The winds, the currents of air or energy that caused the movement toward conception during the intermediate state, dissolve, and the elements of sense perceptions, ego, and the material body begin to form.

Then there are several signs that conception has taken place. For the parents, the signs of conception are that the sexual desire of the woman is satisfied, her heartbeat is accelerated, and her body feels fatigue, languor, and heaviness. This is a sign that the seeds from both male and female regenerative fluids have been held in the womb for conception. It is said that when the woman and man become absorbed together in sexual intercourse, body and mind are blissfully satisfied. The Tibetan textual descriptions of conception are rich and moving, with strong metaphors and images. *The Ambrosia Heart Tantra*, for example, compares this time to arousing fire from rubbing pieces of wood together. It states that the mother's blood may be likened to a flint and the father's sperm to the iron. The consciousness that enters the mixture is like a piece of bark and the embryo like the fire.

According to Tibetan writings, the sperm and ova have specific roles in creating a fetus once intercourse and conception have taken place. Dr. Yeshe Dhonden explains that, according to Tibetan medical literature, the father's sperm contributes bone, brains, spinal cord, and the marrow-like substance running from the brain to the base of the spinal cord.[22] The mother's ova contributes flesh, blood, stomach, intestines, bile, gall bladder, the seminal vesicle, and the five vital organs: the heart, lung, liver, spleen, and kidney.

The elements of earth, water, fire, space, and wind also help form the fetus. The earth element refers to the hard constituents of the body, such as bone, skin, nails, and hair, and it supports the sense of smell. The water element comprises the fluids in the body, such as urine, bile, and blood, and its actions support the sense of taste. The fire element provides the warmth that maintains the body, gives luster to the skin, and the sense of sight. Wind, or air, as it is sometimes called, refers to the currents of energetic substances that perform physical functions such as breathing and swallowing. They also carry the consciousness, as a horse would carry a rider. They are connected with skin and the sense of touch. Space includes all the spaces in the body; it allows for the interaction of all the elements, which enables them to operate. All five elements must be present. Without the earth element there is no formation; without the water element there can be no conglomeration of the embryo or the sperm and the blood; without the fire element there is no maturation; without the wind element there is no growth; and without the space element there is no room for growth.

Conceiving a Boy or Girl

A significant question in every culture is the sex of the child that has been conceived. Some ancient Tibetan teachings indicate that if there is sexual intercourse on the first, third, fifth, seventh, or ninth day of the twelve-day period following menses, a boy will be conceived. On the second, fourth, sixth, eight, tenth, or twelfth day, a girl will be conceived. *The Ambrosia Heart Tantra* likens the end of these twelve days to the closing of a lotus, and thereafter it is said that the sperm is not held in the womb. [23]

Infertility and Malformations

The Ambrosia Heart Tantra includes an entire section on defects in the quality of the ova and sperm, nine in all, which may affect fertility:

> If any of the following defects are present, the sperm and blood are not able to be the seed for an embryo. A wind disorder makes the sperm and blood coarse, dark and thick; a bile disorder makes them sour, yellow and foul-smelling; a phlegm disorder makes them grayish in color, sticky, sweet and cool; a blood disorder makes them putrid; a wind and phlegm disorder makes them runny; a blood and bile disorder makes them pus-like; a phlegm and bile disorder makes them the color of smoke; a wind and bile disorder makes them dry and brittle; a disorder of wind, bile, and phlegm gives them a smell like excrement and urine. [24]

It is interesting to note the way in which the Tibetan analysis of infertility makes use of the senses. Perhaps it is an unorthodox system by Western standards, but, increasingly, Western medicine is faced with challenges of infertility and malformed fetuses. Dr. Dhonden has been invited to lecture and has demonstrated Tibetan methods of diagnosis in hospitals in the United States and other Western countries. Further consideration of complementary approaches across cultures might lead to medical advances or public health policies for prevention as well as treatment of infertility and medical disorders in fetuses and babies.

Rinchen Dolma Taring, in her book *Daughter of Tibet*, writes that "if a couple is not conceiving they can consult a lama to see if it is their karma to have babies. If yes, it is by the blessing of one's deities. There is a charm one can get from a lama to make a woman fertile. This charm can make one have wonderful children, protect old people and children from evil, and make a woman who has not conceived bear children. A lama may also tell a woman to pray to a meditational deity that she has a strong karmic relationship with, and suggest that both she and her husband perform certain rites."[25]

Dr. Lobsang Rapgay provides insight on traditional Tibetan views on conception and infertility. First, he summarizes the different types of infertility, introducing three of the basic premises of the Tibetan medical system: "Infertility can be described in several ways. One is in terms of dysfunctions associated with the energetic systems like *rlung* (pronounced "loong"), which is translated as vital energy, air, *chi*, or *prana*. Dysfunctions of rlung can cause infertility. Dysfunctions of bile or phlegm may be acquired. There are also congenital reasons, things you are born with which make you infertile. Infertility can also be caused by kidney dysfunctions, which affect the urinary tract. Severe infection, inflammation, or dysfunctions can lead to infertility.

"There can also be psychological causes. If you are not psychologically in tune with your body, that can cause infertility. Infertility can also be caused by karmic past life features. Though there is no major dysfunction evident in the bodily realm, somehow you don't conceive," he said, referring to those who, for no apparent reason, have trouble conceiving.

There are traditional Tibetan rituals for overcoming karmic infertility. Because such rituals are often beyond the purview of a medical doctor, a hopeful parent must go to a lama, or a doctor who is a lama, as he knows the elements of ritual or spiritual healing. There are two elements of Tibetan medicine. One is the materialistic element. It deals with the elements of wind, bile, phlegm, earth, and water. This tradition came from China and India.

The other is called tantric medicine, which is ritualistic medicine. It goes beyond the physical and deals with the mind. There are rituals involving deities, rites, and various initiations for virtually all types of disorders. To overcome karmic infertility one must use a ritualistic approach to healing. Through the use of chants, mantras, visualizations, incense, music, bells, and rhythmic vocalizations, Tibetans create a wide range of states of consciousness to be applied for very specific purposes, including the restoration of fertility.

According to Dr. Rapgay, there are also traditional medical treatments of infertility: "Many causes of infertility are medically treated, particularly the rlung one and the psychological one; often the treatment is a combination of medication and ritual, because the problem is not simply organic. A mantra is prescribed on a piece of paper. The mantra is recited over Tibetan paper, rolled into a small ball, encapsulated and given to the patient in pill form once a day for thirty days. I know many Indians, as well as Tibetans, who find that prescription very helpful in conception.

"I feel that those who have psychologically induced infertility have rlung problems, more like psychological neuromuscular fears and anxieties which might inhibit physical functioning. They are not really malfunctioning, but have been inhibited by fears within the psyche. When they take these pills, it is really helpful, both psychologically and spiritually, to dispel anxiety and fears.

"And it works," he concluded, smiling broadly. "Many Indian women take this, and, in addition, a doctor may prescribe myrobalan 18 or saffron 13; these are herbal pills. The idea is first to induce body heat in the woman. When there is enough body heat, conception often occurs. It has to do with body temperature.

"Primarily, one can think of infertility in terms of hot and cold types, for men and women. If the infertility is the cold type, bringing heat to the body is the main cure. That way, in the reproductive process the sperm gets more activity and is able to penetrate more easily. Otherwise its mobility is limited. The hot type of infertility is a little more difficult to treat because this has to do with infection and inflammation within the genital region. This hot or cold physical condition may be the problem rather than the sperm. The hot type is more difficult to assist; the cold type is easier. If the problem is just congestion and the sperm are immobile, all one has to do is produce certain types of appropriate heat. Then the heat removes the congestion and the sperm become a little more mobile. Western medicine has progressed further than Tibetan medicine in treating infection and inflammation, difficulties of the hot type."[26]

Malformations, as well as infertility, are addressed by Dr. Yeshe Dhonden. In his articles on embryology and childbirth, he has written about abnormal births of children with surplus or deficient sense organs or deformities. Tibetan doctors attribute such malformations to harmful winds or energies, impurities of blood, the work of spirits, and the psychic abnormalities of the being's past lives.

Gyatso: A Lama's Perspective

A lama's spiritual viewpoint sheds valuable light on traditional Tibetan birth wisdom. Gyatso, the lama uncle of Palmo and Ngawang, lives in a small village tucked into the hills a few valleys away from Dharamsala. When he is not at the monastery, on retreat, or teaching, Gyatso lives with Ngawang and Palmo and has a great rapport with their three children.

A respected scholar, Gyatso studied Buddhist scripture for many years in a monastery in Tibet before coming to India. He is a vivacious, kind man who loves life and appreciates a diversity of people. He enjoys comparing his life with others, debating philosophical points and practices, and analyzing the conundrums of human behavior. He happily explains the traditional Buddhist texts to those who settle in for an afternoon of storytelling and teaching. While one might expect some natural reticence in a monk during a discussion of childbirth, Gyatso did not hesitate to discuss this topic.

As a monk, Gyatso spoke about conception from a spiritual viewpoint, as it is an event that marks the movement into one's next life and so is an important stage in the rebirth process and the perpetuation of karma. As an important part of this process, Gyatso related how a life, a spiritual being, enters a womb.

"The next life is recorded," Gyatso explained. "My next life is already booked in this life. What comes first in the next life depends on the strength of that recording. Lives can change shape back and forth as situations change. There are many millions of lives, and each recording for the next life is saved in a different part of the stream of consciousness. Certain parts of the recording indicate good rebirth, certain parts indicate less fortunate rebirth. Even if I have all good recordings, and I suddenly do something very, very bad, my record in the negative will increase immediately. My next rebirth could become the very worst."

But, according to Gyatso, this "bad" can be eliminated. There are many different teachings, methods, and practices that provide instruction in this. Some are actually very precise teachings for accumulating merit in this life.

"You know, don't you," Gyatso continued, with a hint of teasing, "that Christians write 'Heaven' with a capital 'H.' But we don't because in Buddhism, heaven is not the ultimate. Attaining enlightenment is the ultimate.

"At conception, when the mother's egg joins with the father's sperm, there are as many minds as all the beings on this planet trying to get into the womb. It isn't competitive. Competition is a Western concept. For us, as Buddhists, it is more as if all these beings are moving about. One's karmic disposition influences them to enter the womb or not. And only one—or two for twins, or more for multiple births—has the karma that draws them to that particular mother and father."

Gyatso reached out in front of him and simulated a swimming motion, imitating all the beings who are milling around the open womb.

"The sperm at that point do not have consciousness. Whichever being has the highest merit will get into a sperm and then all the other sperm do not have a chance to reach consciousness. Buddha said that at each union of a father and mother, there are many sentient beings, as many as all the blades of grass on the planet, trying to get into that life. Luck has nothing to do with it. It is merit and karma that determine which sentient being is drawn into that womb to start a new life. The rest have to seek rebirth somewhere else.

"There are many factors that determine which beings go to which parents. Perhaps a being will not enter one particular womb because these parents are going to produce a child who has a good life, and this being must go into another womb because he or she has the karmic predisposition to work through suffering in the next life. Suffering is part of this being's record and heritage. Of course, you can suffer and still be a person with great merit. Some of the people who suffer the most are great bodhisattvas. Despite their own suffering, bodhisattvas are often ones who are extremely willing to do favors and to help others.

"Now for the parents' view, there is a story about Master Nyima Senge. Before he was born some teachers told his father that he should marry a particular woman. 'If you marry another, you will not get this child,' they said to him, 'but if you marry this woman you will produce a very special child.' That is because the mother and that child are connected."

According to Tibetan tradition, this spiritual connection can be shown to a mother through dreams. There are many stories about mothers who dream certain things when they accept a rebirth. Sometimes the dream is that someone comes to her and says, "Let me come into your room." Or perhaps she dreams that she invites someone into her house, the symbolism being that she is asking someone to come into her womb. Once the mother's womb is entered, what happens next depends on the level of intelligence of the being, whether or not it has high intelligence and, consequently, high awareness, or low intelligence and low awareness.

Gyatso echoed the perceptions of other Tibetans in maintaining that traditionally there was not much preparation for conception, primarily because there was little birth control. Parents accepted children as they came. While there are some married lamas who use physical techniques so they can control birth and decide when to have a child, most people don't practice these advanced techniques. For married couples, it is considered quite natural to want a child; for Tibetans a child is joy, the treasure of the family.

Gyatso also elaborated on the spiritual preparation at the time of conception: "The environment at conception is very important, whether conception is accidental or purposeful. Prayers are very helpful. Meditation can be on love, compassion, or perhaps the nature of mind. From a Buddhist way of seeing, the goodness of male and female union depends on its outcome. It is best to avoid anger, attachment, jealousy, delusions, and other impurities in the relationship. By itself, the union of a mother and father is considered neutral, though it can be positive or even very beneficial. When healthy compassion is present, the union can even contribute to realization of the mind. But copulation can also come prematurely, without readiness; it needs to be entered into with care so it does not have a negative outcome.

"Ideally, male and female energies come into balance in a warm, compassionate, loving, tranquil environment in a gentle way, with mindfulness. It is important that the mind-body not be split, neither the mind engaged in fantasies nor the body in aggressiveness. The quality of gentleness needs to permeate the mind-body to create a good environment for the child to enter. When the egg is fertilized, the mindstream enters into the egg, which becomes a sentient being at the time of conception. The choice of parents is not always a voluntary one. Yet in the intermediate state, imprints and karma ripen and attract us. When there is clarity of mind in life and death, then there is clarity in choice of parents."

In the Tibetan tradition, marriage and reproduction are not sacraments, as they are in Hinduism and Christianity, and the union of a mother and father is neither considered sacred nor offensive. However, sacredness may be perceived in certain tantric spiritual rituals that use intercourse as an important part of spiritual practice. This is a very special practice, and is only performed by thoroughly trained tantric practitioners. In this practice, couples are not intended to conceive; the male does not eject sperm into the woman. Likewise, his consort controls her ovum fluids. In this way, in the Tibetan view, intercourse can be a fundamental form of the highest expression of spiritual integrity and enlightenment— but there is a major distinction between tantric and ordinary intercourse.

Outside these special tantric practices, however, there is no reference or folklore or myth about sacred intercourse. Nor is there any evidence that it is considered profane. It is simply experienced as a natural, biological, earthy function, integrated, as in all Tibetan ways, with the inseparable psychological and spiritual elements of life.

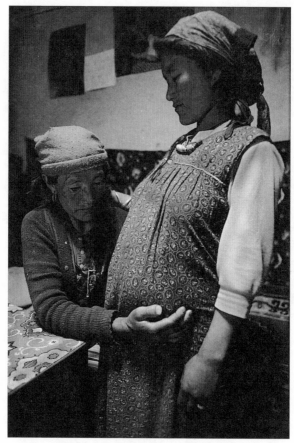

Tibetan mother-to-be with her helper.

3: Gestation

Gems of Tibetan Wisdom through Gestation

◊ *Spirituality grows naturally during the time a child ripens within its mother, and spiritual practice is important to ensure health in the mother and the child.*

◊ *In the Tibetan medical system, pregnancy is confirmed by pulse diagnosis and Tibetan urinalysis, as well as questioning and physical examination.*

◊ *Tibetans make detailed dietary recommendations for the pregnant mother, each based on the relationship of the food to her particular biological system and the stage of development of the fetus.*

◊ *Tibetan medicine warns against alcohol, nicotine, and caffeine during pregnancy, and strongly recommends reducing the use of refined sugar.*

◊ *Tibetan women continue hard work during pregnancy but avoid overly stressful or jarring activities; fathers and extended families are intimately involved with the gestation process.*

◊ *Herbs, massage, and baths are all seen as providing needed nourishment; specific herbs are given to reduce nausea.*

◊ *The meaning of dreams during pregnancy is considered significant and can be linked to later life experience; it also enables the discovery of young incarnate lamas.*

◊ *Each week of gestation holds evolutionary developments, which, when attended to, can guide parents to make choices that assist, rather than hinder, the life unfolding in the womb.*

◊   *If there is difficulty with the pregnancy, a lama can be engaged to do a div-*
ination and to prescribe rituals, arrange a special ceremony, give blessed
pills, or whatever is needed in order to remove any threat to the well-being
of baby or mother.

Tsering

As Tsering walked to the temple, her thick wool shawl almost concealed
the fact that she was seven months pregnant. Tsering and her husband,
Tashi, had recently arrived in Dharamsala, and remained very faithful to
the traditional beliefs and preparations for childbirth. On this morning,
as usual, Tsering went to the temple to do her morning prayer and daily
circumambulation. She pulled out her mala and began to recite the
prayers recommended by a lama for the health of her unborn child. Then
she spun the prayer wheels that encircle the temple—large, ornately
carved, hollow cylinders containing hundreds of handwritten prayers. Her
right hand moved like the flap of a paddle wheel, generating endless
prayers inside the wheel.

Entering the temple, she came to a room where dozens of maroon-
robed monks were lined up and chanting with great concentration and
intensity. She stopped and listened to their low, rhythmic voices, which
generated waves of reverberating sound. The monks sat cross-legged, in
rows, on red cushions before low prayer tables, chanting in unison and
swaying slightly under the direction of the chant master. A sudden clang
of hand cymbals blended in with the chanting. The heavy smell of incense
permeated the wood, wool, walls, and religious icons: the tankas, statues
of deities, and Tibetan texts.

Tsering was both energized and comforted by the chanting, the
rhythm, and the sounds of bells, horns, gongs, and drums. The complex
woven patterns of vibrations created a sense of power that could be felt, as
well as heard. With a protective hand on her stomach, she sensed that her
baby could feel it as well. Although she was in Dharamsala, she could
almost imagine that she was back at home in Tibet. Outside, she continued her circumambulation, feeling a deep sense of protection and well-
being. She felt certain that the chanting of the monks and her own

prayers were a very strong positive force when concentrated on the health of her baby.

Gestation is that enriching time during which a baby grows inside its mother. In the nine months of pregnancy, the fetus transforms from a meeting of egg and sperm to a whole being with a mind and physical body suitable for life outside the womb. The bond between mother and baby grows strong and deep as they spend twenty-four hours a day together. The baby becomes accustomed to the mother's movements, her voice, her feelings, and the love she is sending to her womb. Concurrently, the mother becomes accustomed to carrying the baby, to caring for it, to incorporating it into her life. In the Tibetan tradition, this time is also associated with increased spirituality, as well as concerns for physical health and well-being.

Spiritual Practice During Pregnancy

As a lama, Gyatso observed a heightening of spirituality in women during pregnancy. "Wherever there is a time of solitude, such as the growth of inner attention during pregnancy," Gyatso noted, "there is a tendency to turn to spirituality. Women know they must ultimately give birth alone, even if they are surrounded by family and friends. In the Tibetan tradition, spiritual practice is considered very important in order to ensure the safety of the pregnancy, the health of the mother and the child. A series of spiritual activities—rites, rituals, reciting mantras—are carried on constantly when a woman is pregnant."

Tibetan couples turn to their spiritual leaders for guidance during this time, as they do during every stage of the birth process. Sometimes they make offerings to monks or nuns who will recite mantras and prayers on their behalf. One well-known mantra is from Padmasambhava, the Vajra Guru mantra: OM AH HUM VAJRA GURU PADMA SIDDHI HUM, (or OM AH HUNG BENZA GURU PEMA SIDDHI HUNG, as pronounced by Tibetans). The full meaning of any mantra is complex, for it works at many levels. This one represents the transformative blessings of the body, speech, and mind of all the buddhas: diamond-like purity and strength, wisdom, knowledge, compassion, skillful means, enlightened speech, and realization of enlightenment. [27]

These prayers may take place at the couple's home, or their prayers may be recited at the temple. The number of monks or nuns who recite the prayers is less important than the mindfulness, motivation, and number of recitations of each prayer. The monks and nuns chant the text, mantras, or prayers over and over again, until the words vibrate with a sense of protection and well-being. If there is difficulty in the couple's life, or if the pregnancy is not going well, a couple may ask a lama to do a divination and prescribe for them particular ritualistic activities. As part of the purification process, it is believed that these rituals will help cleanse the mother's personal karma, as well as that of her unborn child. Often the prayers and rituals prescribed for the mother and father to repeat and enact will be related to the goddess Tara: either Green Tara, as discussed in the "Conception" chapter, or to White Tara, a feminine enlightened being who gives power and support. Prayers and rituals conducted at the monastery or nunnery are longer, more complex, and draw on long years of training in a variety of skills and methods which focus spiritual energy.

Long-life rituals, often conducted by a highly esteemed visiting rinpoche, are also commonly prescribed. A long-life ceremony, in which the mantras focus on cleansing, health, and longevity, is usually held in the largest room of the temple, which is ornately and colorfully prepared with brocade banners in many forms. Although the ceremony may differ from one place to another, the rinpoche, lamas, and monks chant sacred texts, accompanied by horns, bells, and drums. Those who come, of all ages, are dressed in their best, and each carries a *kata*, a white silk scarf, to be presented to the rinpoche, each in their turn. The rinpoche then blesses them, and perhaps their mala as well, often with a touch, nearly always with a warm smile, and places the kata over the back of their bowed neck so that it hangs down over their heart. A colorful blessed protection cord, to be tied around the neck or arm and worn afterward, is also given each participant by the lama or rinpoche, and a monk pours a small amount of blessed water into each person's palm to drink.

In Tibetan healing rituals, an effigy, created to represent a destructive spirit, is cast away to stop the spirit from harming a person. In the case of an unborn child, the lama may make an effigy of the spirit who seems to be upsetting or causing harm to the baby. First, a lama discerns which specific spirit is causing the trouble. He then molds a small statue, usually out of barley dough, in the image of that spirit. Following a ritual, which may include stylized movement as well as protective chants, the effigy is cast away, in the belief that all its dangerous qualities are thereby removed from the child or patient. For pregnancy and birth, this ritual may be performed during each stage of development, deterring spirits that might disturb the natural process of gestation.

In some cases, the family's oracle, or divine seer, might answer questions about a particular child by going into a trance. Those who are chosen as oracles are appointed by a monastic committee, based on tests of their capacity to know what is true and to offer advice based on their visions of the future.

It is common for a lama to prescribe that parents-to-be give alms and perform charitable acts such as feeding animals or giving food to the poor, especially needy children. A woman may buy food, sweets, or chocolates and go to a place where there are many poor children and provide their meals for the day. Another common prescription is feeding birds. The prescription may vary during the nine months, not because of stages in pregnancy, but because of difficulties with the pregnancy or astrological or divination readings for the child—especially for high lamas or, in earlier times, royal families. In this case, special prayers might be said at the monastery. The mother and father are advised to practice these rituals together because it is believed that the child inside is already aware of this attention. In the same way, the father is encouraged to show much love, compassion, and care toward mother and baby.

Diet During Pregnancy

As in Western pregnancy care, Tibetan care during pregnancy emphasizes special nutritional considerations for the mother-to-be. Increasingly, the Western medical community is discovering the crucial link between a woman's diet during pregnancy and the lifelong health of the unborn child.[28] As the umbilical cord connects the mother and child, it is only logical that anything ingested by the mother will have a direct line to the baby: a direct cause and effect situation. This belief has been reflected in Tibetan tradition and literature for centuries, and modern Western recommendations and cautions about alcohol, caffeine, nicotine, and sugar, for example, bear a striking resemblance to this Tibetan wisdom.

The Tibetan view of diet during pregnancy follows from the belief that preparation for birth is a natural process, not that special medical care is needed prior to the birth of a child. However, most Tibetan midwives and doctors do impart basic dietary guidelines, which are common knowledge in most Tibetan homes. Tibetan dietary recommendations are fine-tuned according to the stage of gestation. For the first six months, any food that may have a purgative effect is reduced. Women are cautioned against eating foods that are severely acidic, fermented, or very spicy. For instance, yogurt is fine, but eating fermented cheese is discouraged.

Alcohol or any other fermented food is not recommended. These are considered toxic in the sense that they produce fermentation, which can produce unhealthy bacteria. Even ancient Tibetan texts warn that liquor is harmful to a growing fetus. They state that a woman should have no alcohol at all while pregnant as there are so many parts of the fragile development process it can negatively affect.

There are a few ancient Tibetan traditions that advocate the ingestion of small amounts of alcohol. Some women drink a little whiskey or rum, sometimes mixed with hot butter, from the time they are pregnant to a few weeks after birth, in the belief that the alcohol will make the uterus heal more quickly. But most Tibetan women today do not feel the potential benefits to the uterus are worth the risk to the baby.

The consumption of caffeine is also discouraged. Again, it is interesting to note that modern studies show that the toxic impact of caffeine on unborn babies is double its effect on adults. Too much refined sugar is not recommended, though sweets in the form of fruit and honey are encouraged. Also very cold food or too much roughage in raw food is not recommended, as these are particularly difficult to digest. The mother-to-be is also encouraged to avoid rich, greasy food, like pork, and foods like sausages that are made from the intestines of an animal.

Dr. Dolma writes of the eighteenth week of gestation, "The mother observes a certain diet so that she can give a beautiful appearance to the child. She should avoid or reduce intake of spices that make the mouth hot, like chilies and black pepper, and food that creates heat. From the cold types of food, she should avoid buttermilk and whey. One should stop eating all artificially processed food. This is the time when most of the flesh and the fat are forming so what the mother eats is very important. Many babies are born with scaly skin that looks like snake skin or like a fish; the reason for this defect is that the mother has not observed a correct diet at this formative time." The skin is said to cover the muscles, the lymphatic system, the tendons and ligaments in the twenty-first week, and hair is said to begin its growth in the twenty-third week.

In the later weeks of pregnancy, a woman's body may instinctively reject certain foods. Fresh foods are recommended, but Tibetans generally prepare them in soups. Heavy grains and heavy beans are not recommended. These are very compact and therefore difficult to assimilate or break down. If heavy foods are eaten, it is believed that the extra effort in digesting them takes away energy from the fetus. Consequently, the Tibetan diet during the last few months of pregnancy consists of many hearty soups, with chicken, vegetables, and light grains such as barley.

The Tibetan tradition addresses a woman's experience of unusual cravings while pregnant. Early in the pregnancy, a woman often craves bitter, sour foods. And indeed, this craving is encouraged. There is a belief in a beneficial quality of foods and herbs with a bitter taste in the first months of pregnancy. This tradition has a biological basis. What the Tibetans refer to as the heat, or bile, system is considered more active during the first stages of pregnancy. This condition may cause headaches or nausea, so a food that has a cooling effect, such as sour or bitter foods, is consequently balancing and therapeutic, and so reduces or eliminates what Westerners call "morning sickness" in the first three months.

Physical Activity During Pregnancy

While exercise is encouraged during pregnancy, it is not recommended that a woman engage in activities that are too stressful or strenuous. As the child begins to form and the woman begins to feel the weight of the fetus, massage is recommended, especially with sesame oil. Massage is considered a form of nourishment, as are regular baths. Cleanliness, a sort of purification, is considered important, and it is recommended to keep as clean as possible and bathe frequently.

Moderate exercise is recommended throughout pregnancy, especially a great deal of walking. As is often the way in Tibetan tradition, physical, emotional, and spiritual care merge in the course of an activity. Often mothers-to-be take most of their exercise circumambulating a temple. In the same way, a caution to refrain from lifting heavy objects is said in the same breath as a warning to avoid negative thoughts and speech, anger, or overexcitement.

Stages of Development of the Fetus

Ancient and modern Tibetan texts describe specific stages in the development of the fetus. There are striking similarities between these ancient medical teachings and the evolving Western medical definitions for these stages.

The ancient book *Illustrated Principles and Practices of Tibetan Medicine*, dating from the eleventh century, may be the oldest text in the world to describe the gestation process in medical terms.[29] In the style typical of Tibetan books, its pages are loose, piled atop one another with no binding to hold them together. The illustrations are painted like a series of tankas: traditional, minutely detailed, and highly stylized. The writing is in Tibetan script, which Lobsang Rapgay translated for me.

Three Stages of Growth

The section on human embryology begins with a description of the three stages of human growth in the womb: the fish phase, the turtle phase, and the pig phase. According to historians, this text provides evidence that by the eleventh century a culture had identified these three evolutionary processes. Interestingly, twentieth-century Western obstetrics now also speaks of the distinct natures of the first, second, and third trimesters of pregnancy.

Later Tibetan texts agree. Dr. Dolma, in her *Lectures on Tibetan Medicine*, echoes the concept that the fetus grows through three basic evolutionary stages. And Namkhai Norbu, in his book *On Birth and Life: A Treatise on Tibetan Medicine*, also describes these three stages.

Norbu gives a detailed description of the three stages in language that explains the synthesis of the physical and spiritual elements of the transitions. According to his writings, the first night after conception the sperm and the ovum are united but not yet amalgamated one with the other; they are together like separate peas in a pod. Between the two, the life energy and the mind of the unborn child are firmly held. Soon thereafter, the life energy and the mind mesh with their male and female origins. This union emerges as a very fine web, or thread, of life, which becomes the basis for continued growth. If this thread of life is straight, it foretells long life; if it curves towards the right or left then life may be easily interrupted. If it is pointed downward, the life will be brief. For the first six days, the embryo's development is fostered by the intermixing of the male and female elements. In all, the embryo requires four weeks to take shape and another nine weeks to complete the first stage of its development.[30] The fish phase is the first thirteen weeks of gestation when the embryo resembles a fish.

After three months, Namkhai Norbu notes, the mother's belly is enlarged. At about the fifth month, the lower part of the uterus is a finger's breadth beneath the navel. During this phase the orifices of the newly forming body take shape and the limbs elongate like those of a turtle. This time is therefore called the phase of the turtle.

About six months after conception, the bottom of the uterus is more or less a finger's width above the navel, and from month to month it rises higher. By the ninth month, the uterus has arrived two finger's breadths beneath the sternum. Through the ninth month, the uterus lowers one or two finger's widths and seems to enlarge a little. During this period the fetus has finished taking shape and has grown hair on its head and body. This last phase is called the pig phase.

Thirty-nine Weeks of Development: Traditional Version

Illustrated Principles and Practices also gives a detailed look at the Tibetan view of the week-by-week development of the fetus.

The development in the first week is portrayed in a tanka that shows the elemental forces that shape the fetus: bile, water, and the elements—earth, water, fire, air, and space. The mother and the father, the ovum and the sperm, are mixed and interacting during this time.

In the second week, the embryo is circular in form, and by the fifth week the embryo's navel makes a distinct connection to the mother's navel in terms of the fetal shape. In the sixth week the spinal cord is being formed. In the corresponding tanka, the sensory organs, the eyes, and the head are barely discernable.

At the eighth week the head is more clearly formed. And at the ninth week the stomach and the upper body forms. This is still the fish stage, or the first stage of evolution, during which the fetus is like a sea creature living in the sea. By the tenth week the shoulders and hips have formed. And in the eleventh week the nine orifices form—the eyes, ears, nose, genitals, and mouth.

In the twelfth week the five organs start to form: the heart, lungs, liver, spleen, and the left and right kidneys. In the thirteenth week the six hollow organs start to form: the stomach, the intestines, the large intestines, the gall bladder, the uterus, or the seminal vesicles for a boy, and the urinary bladder.

At the beginning of the turtle phase, in the fourteenth week, the thighs, legs, and extremities begin to form. Then the fingers and the nails begin to appear in the fifteenth week. In the sixteenth week, the nervous system begins to manifest. This is the mechanism that allows the fetus to connect the internal workings of its organs with what the outside of its body experiences. The muscles form during the eighteenth week. And in the nineteenth week, the lymphatic system and tendons and ligaments grow.

In the twenty-first week, the skin forms. The skin protects the body; prior to that it's very tender. At this point, the ears and nose, which had developed previously, are finally open. And the pores begin to open as well.

The final stage of evolution of the fetus is the pig phase. The twenty-fifth week is particularly important, as this is when breathing begins. At this point, there is a caution in the text, which indicates the mother should not lie on her belly as the child's nose and mouth might be pressed. If she rests on her knees and then lies forward, the baby's six senses will become impaired. And if the mother bends her leg in an awkward way, then the child's arms will feel that pressure and may break or cover its own mouth or nose.

In the twenty-sixth and twenty-seventh week, the mind begins to function and the baby can sense and interpret things to some degree. From the twenty-seventh to the thirtieth week, the sensory organs become sharper. In the thirty-first through thirty-fifth weeks, the total person begins to function.

By the thirty-sixth week, the organism experiences emotions of grief and dissatisfaction, and by then in the thirty-seventh week, it experiences repulsion. This is when the baby begins to feel the desire to escape. The thirty-seventh to the thirty-ninth weeks are the final phase. The fetus prepares itself to come out.

Thirty-nine Weeks of Development: Contemporary Version

Dr. Lobsang Dolma's collection of essays called *Lectures on Tibetan Medicine* also outlines the weekly stages of fetal development. It is interesting to note that the more modern Tibetan medical view bears a close resemblance to the descriptions in ancient Tibetan texts.

Dr. Dolma has written that during the first week after conception, the rlung—the wind, air, or breath containing vital energy—takes effect in the fetus.[31] The rlung is the life-sustaining energetic flow that is primarily responsible for all natural processes in human beings. The function of the rlung is to completely mix the five elements, the subtle energies of the mother in the ovum, and those of the father in the sperm; and to give solidity to the embryo that is being formed.

By the third week, a rlung called the Treasury of Vital Energy comes into action and the embryo becomes even more solid than before. In the fourth week, this hardening and solidifying continues. At this point, the mother's womb, which had been growing big, begins to recede and grow thinner. It is the same rlung as before, but it is now working more intensely. The belly of the mother will be protruding at the center and will become depressed at each side. This is because the form of the embryo has become elongated and is vertical in the uterus.

By the fifth week, the embryo has more firmness, like a piece of growing wood. It does not bend as much as before. At this point, although the sexual organ has not been formed, the sexual power, or the energy, of possessing a male or female sexual organ exists. At this phase it is called the Hardness Is Now Changing because this is the moment in which the channels, the veins, and the different airs and spaces in the organism will be formed.

From then on, new elements are formed each week, such as new channels, new veins, and different rlung. Dr. Dolma explains that the first part of the body to be formed is the navel. From the navel, three main channels are formed. They are the channel of life (the foundation of consciousness), the channel of air or breath, and the channel of strength.

During the seventh week the main, or central, channel grows upward, and sixteen fetus-sized finger-breadths upward from the navel, the heart is formed. Then, at the level of the heart, a center of channels is formed which is called the Dharmachakra or the Wheel of Dharma. This coincides with the eighth vertebra in the child's back.

The central channel continues to grow upward, and when it reaches the same level as the first vertebrae, it is at the throat. At the throat, the center of channels called the Wheel of Enjoyment is formed. And then the central channel grows upward until it reaches what would be the crown of the head. At that point it forms another wheel of channels, which is called the Wheel of Great Bliss. When this wheel has been formed, the five sense organs begin to take shape.

During the ninth and tenth weeks, the upper part of the body can be distinguished from the lower part of the body, although the limbs have still not come out. Then during the ninth week, the shoulders are formed. They become pronounced, as do the hips. The bones of the shoulders and the hips take their characteristic form. At that point the fetus still looks like a fish. In the eleventh week, the openings in the organs begin to form.

At this point, all the veins and nerves that connect the organs inside the body, as well as the ones that we see closest to the surface, are formed. Up to this point, the fetus does not have a consciousness of its body. But in the seventeenth week, the navel rlung starts to function. And this is the starting point for the child to begin to experience its body. The action of this rlung is that through its influence, veins are formed connecting the stomach with the liver through which basic nutrients can be assimilated by the liver. Then the spleen and other vessels for the purification of the blood are formed. At this point the face looks like that of a turtle.

During the eighteenth week, the rlung that is called the Stainless Vital Energy of Life force starts its action. This rlung is absolutely pure, without any type of contamination. Around that time, the mother can give special attention to a diet that will nurture the development of beautiful flesh, skin, and hair, as discussed earlier.

The rlung that starts to function in the nineteenth week is called the Extremely Vital Energy. This means that it is immaterial, it is not evident. This rlung imbues the different parts of the body with the ability to perform their specific functions, such as moving the tongue, creating saliva, and so forth.

During the twentieth week, the Extremely Stable Energy starts to firm up the bones, which had until this time been flexible. Inside the bones the marrow starts to form. Four classifications of bones begin to form: first, the long bones, such as the femur or thigh bones, and the bones in the arm; then the ribs; then the round bones, or the bones of the joints; and then the round bones that float within the body space, like the skull, the shoulder blades, and the kneecap.

In the twenty-second week, the wind called the Invincible Vital Energy starts to work. Blood and water will begin to circulate, and menstrual blood will come if the fetus is female. Also, the sensory organs like the eyes finally become defined. We can then see the eyeballs, the coloring, the iris, and so forth. Then in the twenty-third week, the Vital Energy of Complete Grasping starts to function. All the hairs start to grow, and the nails become hard.

At this point, the mother may have acidity in her stomach and heartburn. But this is not a sickness, it is just a result of the growth of the fetus. If the mother is diagnosed at this time, she might be told she has some disease of the phlegm and be given medicine to warm up the body. This is not healthful for the child, however, as it impairs the growth of the child's hair.

In the twenty-fourth week, the rlung called Ever Moving Vital Energy causes the fetus to experience feelings in relationship to all the inner organs. There is a heightened relationship between what the mother does and how it affects the fetus. If the mother jumps heavily on her feet, the fetus may feel anxious. Or if the mother lays on her belly, or presses the belly too hard at the sides, then the fetus may feel a localized pain in certain organs. Consequently, in order that a fetus will not be injured or have a problem with its liver and eyesight, the mother should be cautious in her behavior. At this point it is especially important that she abstain from any intoxicants like wine, beer, or hard liquor.

In the twenty-sixth week, the Energy Established in Previous Lives begins. The child's awareness becomes very clear and it can see its former lives. It can see if it was a pure being or an ordinary being and what type of birth it had in past lives. And then from the twenty-seventh to thirtieth weeks, gradually all the different sense organs, which are already functioning, develop further and ripen.

In those four weeks, three kinds of rlung work in unison: the Vital Energy, the Flower Garland Vital Energy, and the Iron-Gate Vital Energy. Through the action of these three working together, the channels of the body—the veins, nerves, and the arteries—become more developed. Especially the five main veins in the heart. The child therefore has mobility. The arms and legs can be stretched.

From the thirtieth to thirty-fifth weeks, the child and its mother do not coincide in their states. Sometimes the mother is healthy and the child is unhealthy, or if the child is healthy, the mother will not feel well. Mother and child begin to experience dissimilarities.[32] At this point, the child has already grown to its full extent.

During the thirty-sixth week, the child starts to feel that the womb is a dirty environment rather than a nurturing home. At this point, there arise in the mind of the child five types of perceptions that strengthen its wish to be born so it can get out of that environment. These wishes to leave the environment come first from the perception of uncleanliness; second, from a perception of a foul smell; third, from the experiences of darkness or a feeling of being imprisoned; fourth, from a feeling of uncomfortableness. The fifth perception is dissatisfaction; the child's mind is unhappy. The unborn baby expresses its feeling of wanting to leave the womb by moving its arms and entire body. At this point, the mother should visit the midwife or doctor regularly for examination.

The child's growing desire to be out of the womb prepares the way for leaving behind the place the baby has spent so many weeks growing and developing. Being born is the natural next step for the child, not the harsh separation from the warmth and security of the womb that birth is often characterized to be.

There are some differences between the eleventh-century Illustrated Principles and Practices and Dr. Dolma's twentieth-century book: the ancient text uses illustration to elaborate on descriptions, while the notes on Dr. Dolma's lectures give more textual description. However, there is a strong resemblance in their basic descriptions of week-by-week growth. Both texts are in accord regarding the circumstances of the fetus when the time to leave the womb nears. At this point, the fetus is already feeling that it wants to get out, to move on. The separation is easy. Both the mother and the baby want the baby out and on to begin the next stage.

Determination of Sex

According to Tibetan tradition, there are special signs to determine the sex of a baby. If the left side of the mother's stomach is higher during pregnancy, this indicates the child is a girl. If the baby is a boy, the right side of the stomach is higher, milk comes from the right breast, and the mother likes to lean to the right when sitting or standing. They also say it is a son when the bulge of the mother's stomach is rather pointed and high, her body feels light, and she dreams of the birth of a boy. Dreams of horses and elephants or of meeting men also signify that the child is a boy.

Tankas in the Illustrated Principles and Practices show that if the fetus lies mainly on the right side it will be a boy, if on the left side, a girl. And if it's in the middle, it will be twins.

Folklore of Childbirth

The bookstore at the Library of Tibetan Works and Archives in Dharamsala is a good source for recently published books that address various aspects of Tibetan culture and philosophy. When I was visiting Dharamsala, the bookstore was run by Norbu Chophel Kharitsang, a folklorist and scholar of traditional culture who has published two books on traditional customs, folklore, and superstitions. He interviewed many older Tibetans in the area and in Tibetan settlements to preserve a record of the old ways before they were lost or diluted. Norbu had found that the event of childbirth highlights many Tibetan beliefs and customs that surface in the culture. Some of the most important and pervasive of Tibetan beliefs surround the significant event of birthing.[33]

"In the Tibetan tradition childbirth is full of superstitions," he related. "For instance, nine months and ten days is the usual period of gestation, but some Tibetans believe that, if by chance, a horse walks over a pregnant woman, or if she gets under a horse, or even if its shadow falls on her, she will undergo what is known as *Ta-dip*. *rTa-Grib* is the actual spelling: *rTa* means horse and *Grib* is pronounced as *dip*, a sort of pollution, an invisible darkness. The outcome of this is that the woman will remain pregnant for twelve months, the length of time a mare gestates."

Norbu had an array of traditional beliefs and superstitions to share. He had read of cases in which the child in the womb disappeared after a crash of thunder. Some Tibetans believe that thunder represents the cries of a dragon, and it is a dragon that takes the child away from the womb. Some believe they can determine the sex of the baby while it is still in the womb in several ways. They may determine this by seeking the help of a reincarnated lama's clairvoyant insight and prophesying powers. Also the mother can tell by the discharge of blood. If she discharges blood before a delivery, it will be a boy. If there is no discharge of blood, it will be a girl. The blood that is discharged is called *gDung-Khrag* which means lineage blood. It is called this because a lineage breaks up when the family has no male descendants. (Like many other cultures, family lineage in Tibetan society is patrilineal, passed down through the sons.) In traditional folklore, the pregnancy itself can be foretold in dreams. If a woman dreams of snakes or frogs, it means she is pregnant. Snakes in particular are associated with fertility, so for a woman to dream of a snake signifies her own fertility, specifically a new pregnancy.

Dreams During Pregnancy

In the Tibetan tradition, dreams during pregnancy may carry import regarding the health and personality of the baby. In many cases, mothers will report a significant dream during pregnancy. However, it is often difficult to interpret or determine whether these dreams are truly connected to the baby or not. Many dreams are considered to have links to the unborn child. People say that if a child is destined to have a good life, the parents, especially the mother, will frequently have auspicious dreams in the latter part of the night, and the mother will experience a newfound joy. Generally these dreams are of picking and eating fruit; of certain auspicious objects, such as a white conch shell; of wearing fine jewelry or clothing; of seeing and receiving representations of the body, speech, and mind of the enlightened ones, buddhas and bodhisattvas; of sunrise or day dawning; and of playing musical instruments.

According to Tibetan tradition, these dreams may often be very simply interpreted as either auspicious or inauspicious. For instance, a woman may have auspicious dreams when she is carrying an exceptional baby, such as a reincarnated teacher or rinpoche. If the child is to have misfortune in life, the parents will have inauspicious dreams: they may dream of an event such as falling off a cliff; of sunset; of darkness; of wandering without ornaments or jewelry on an empty, deserted plain; of arguing with others; of crying; or of being carried by water. Also the mother may become unhappy or depressed for no apparent reason. In the case of an inauspicious dream, the parents or the mother may go to a lama, who would then do a divination and prescribe rituals or prayers. This would then balance out any potential negativity.

This belief in the significance of dreams is strong in the Tibetan community in Dharamsala. Lhamo, Palmo, and Tsering recalled very detailed dreams, both auspicious and inauspicious, while pregnant.

Lhamo had unusual, prophetic dreams while carrying two of her children: "With this little one, Lhakpa, I had many dreams about my spiritual teacher. Mostly he would ask me, 'How are you? Are you doing your mantras and practices?' I would tell him, and he would encourage me. That was the constant theme of those dreams. And when my sister was pregnant, I had the dream of fruits. I did not yet know she was pregnant, but when I had this dream in which I was offering fruits, I woke up and told my husband that I thought my sister was pregnant. When you offer fruits or eggs in a dream, it symbolizes belonging, so you know that a baby who belongs to you is coming. After awhile I received a letter from my sister that she was pregnant, so I thought that maybe these dreams were true. Oftentimes they are.

"With my first baby, I dreamed that there were two of my husband, two Dorjes. I woke up and told him that we were going to have someone extra in our family because I dreamed two of him. And I thought I would have a boy. Another Dorje. But still I was surprised when I actually did! Up to that point, I had been thinking it was going to be a girl. In fact, Dorje had dreamed of snakes which made me know I was pregnant with this baby. Dorje dreamed that there was a big snake lying between us, and Dorje felt warm. One night, he tried to hit the snake in his dream, and he jostled me by mistake. I woke up, and he said he was trying to move the snake he was dreaming about. He had this dream twice. One time the snake bit his toe. I told Dorje that some spirits must be on their way, or maybe I was pregnant. And then a little later I went to Delek Hospital and they did a test and told me I was two-and-a-half months pregnant. Which means I would have been about one-and-a-half months pregnant when the dream came. Because of the snake dream I came to think I was going to be pregnant—especially as it bit him, and because he felt warm."

Tsering had also experienced revelatory dreams while pregnant: "When I was pregnant with my daughter in Tibet, the one who was killed in the cross-fire in Lhasa, I had some foreboding dreams. And then later, when she was just seven years old, she was in the main square in Lhasa at just the wrong time and was killed by a stray Chinese bullet. We thought it was a terrible accident and wondered what was in her karma to make that happen to her. But now I remember those bad dreams during my pregnancy with her. At the time I thought they were nightmares, but now as I think back, they were inauspicious dreams.

"But with this baby," Tsering settled her hand on her protruding belly, "I've had the most auspicious dreams! Just last week I dreamed of a whole banquet of fruit! And when I first discovered I was pregnant, I had a very vivid dream in which I was in a beautiful room, well-decorated and warm. I was lured right into it. And I was inviting someone to come join me in this beautiful room: I couldn't tell who it was, but I felt it was someone I was very close to. Soon after, I realized I was pregnant. That is a very typical dream, inviting someone into a room. It symbolizes inviting someone into your womb. And sure enough I had invited this baby into me."

The Tibetan interpretation of these dreams is passed along to new generations in several ways, often simply as a part of growing up and being part of the community. Beginning in school, children are taught the significance of dreams. And dream interpretation is also passed on by other teachers and elders of the community. Tibetan books often discuss dreams and their meanings. Many stories, poems, and tales of deities and spirits feature elements of these beliefs as well.

Reincarnation

In the Tibetan tradition, dreams are often a way for a person, or an unborn baby, to bridge life in this world with other lives. For instance, in the twenty-sixth week of pregnancy, it is believed that the fetus begins to remember its past lives. At this point, the mother may experience unusual dreams, as if they belonged to somebody else. There may be different settings that seem unfamiliar, yet somehow important. A mother who attends to these dreams may have hints about her child's earlier lives and calling or the child's purpose in this life.

Normally, when lamas are conceived, their mother has a special dream, such as the dream experienced by Queen Mayadevi, the Buddha's mother. She had prayed in a previous life to be the mother of a buddha. When the Buddha decided that it was time for him to be born from the womb of Queen Mayadevi, she dreamt that a six-tusked white elephant entered her womb through her right side at midnight. Upon inquiring about this of the Brahmin soothsayers, they prophesied that a son had been conceived in her who would become a great universal emperor if he followed the life of a settled householder. But if he were instead to follow the life of a wandering monk, he would become a perfect one, a buddha.[34]

Dreams continue to be an important tool for lamas in determining where a beloved rinpoche has reincarnated in his next life. A great rinpoche will often have a dream before he dies, indicating the direction in which his successors should look to find his reincarnation. The use of dreams as tools to discover reincarnations is not confined to Tibet or Asia. Vicki MacKenzie's book *Reincarnation: The Boy Lama* describes the unusual situation of a Tibetan monk who was well-known in the Western world, Lama Yeshe, and his rebirth in the form of a young Spanish boy, Lama Osel. When Lama Zopa, Lama Yeshe's main disciple, was diligently searching for Lama Yeshe's reincarnation, he used dreams as an important tool to lead him to the right child.

In one vivid dream, Lama Yeshe declared to Lama Zopa that he was about to take another human form. In a later dream, Lama Zopa saw a small child with bright penetrating eyes, crawling on the floor of a meditation room. This child was male and a Westerner. When Lama Zopa first saw Lama Osel, it was exactly the scene he had seen in his dream.

Deeply curious, he sought out and found the baby's mother and questioned her thoroughly on any dreams she had while she was pregnant with this baby. She said there was one in particular in which she had been in a large cathedral where Lama Yeshe was giving teachings to a huge crowd. Many were Christians and they were all kneeling rather than sitting cross-legged in the Tibetan style. Along with everyone else, she approached Lama Yeshe to receive his blessing and when he touched her she felt as though pure water, blissful golden-white water, was pouring through her, purifying her. It also turned out that the baby had been conceived on exactly the day that Lama Zopa had his first dream of Lama Yeshe announcing he was going to be reborn.[35]

A British woman named Greta Jensen had a dream that helped find the reincarnation of Zong Rinpoche in the Kulu-Manali area of the Indian Himalayas. She was a close disciple of the previous incarnation of Rinpoche. She dreamt of a small child, full of golden light radiating from within. The child was playing outside a whitewashed stone house with a river behind it and the Himalayas in the distance. It turned out that the house in which the reincarnated boy was discovered was exactly the one in her dream. The boy's mother, Tashi Yangdzom, often dreamt of being blessed by the Dalai Lama when she was pregnant. Before giving birth she also visited a lama who told her the child would be an important person.[36]

The fourteenth, and present, Dalai Lama, was discovered in a similar way, though he was found by visions rather than by dreams. As he describes in his book *My Land and My People*, the Regent responsible for finding him went to a sacred lake in Tibet to receive a vision of where to begin the search. In 1935, the Tibetan Wood Hog year, the regent went to the sacred lake of Lhamoi Latso at Chokhorgyal, about ninety miles southwest of Lhasa. The people of Tibet believe that visions of the future can be seen in the waters of this lake. There are many such holy lakes in Tibet, but Lhamoi Latso is the most celebrated of them all. Sometimes the visions are said to appear in the form of letters, and sometimes as pictures of places and future events.

After several days in prayer and meditation, the Regent saw the vision of three Tibetan letters—*Ah*, *Ka*, and *Ma*—followed by a picture of a monastery with roofs of jade green and gold and a house with turquoise tiles. A detailed description of these visions was written down and kept a strict secret.[37] The Regent followed these visions and was led right to the Dalai Lama's house in the small town of Taktser in Eastern Tibet. A series of tests were then conducted to verify that they had, indeed, found the right little boy.[38]

There are many accounts, both written and anecdotal, of Tibetans using dreams and visions as a primary tool to locate reincarnations of lamas, rinpoches, and other special people. Increasingly, dreams and visions to find reincarnations are appearing to Western Tibetan Buddhist practitioners as well. Given that pregnancy and birth are seen as a time of heightened spiritual awareness, the information in dreams takes on heightened significance.

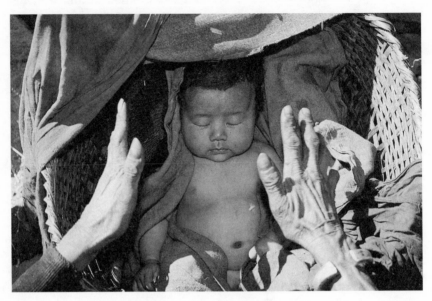

Newborn Tibetan child is welcomed into the world.

4: Birthing

Gems of Tibetan Wisdom in Birthing

◊   *Each birth connects lives from beginningless time and boundless space.*

◊   *Birth as a human being is a treasured privilege with unique opportunities to experience reality, grow in knowledge, and develop spiritually, as well as to express a universal responsibility to all life.*

◊   *Birth is a natural process, and there are natural ways to ease labor and delivery.*

◊   *The whole extended family is involved in assisting with a birth.*

◊   *Purposeful rituals at the time of birth honor the event and evoke qualities in a child's development that are valued in the culture.*

◊   *Everything has a cause, and each birth is part of an ongoing continuity in the cycle of experience through eons; there are an infinite number of rebirths.*

Palmo

As usual, Palmo spent the early part of the morning circumambulating the temple and praying for the health of her baby. Her mother had told her about women in Tibet who performed all their normal chores, including carrying heavy pails of milk to market, right up to the time they gave birth. Her mother also told her that walking exercises the child—makes the child's body supple and provides it with a firm, upright body—and paves the way for a quick and easy birth. Although she was nine months pregnant and clearly ready to give birth at any moment, she heeded her mother's advice and planned to continue her routine until the day the baby was born.

She walked around the temple once, circumambulating it in a clockwise direction, the way the sun goes, as is the custom, and spun all the prayer wheels she passed. Then she took off her shoes before quietly entering the temple. She lit incense and left an offering of several rupees. Concentrating her energy on the safe delivery and birth of her baby, she prayed. She also made an offering of some money to the temple caretaker to say a good-luck prayer. She then gathered up her shawl to go home.

During her pregnancy, Palmo had been very careful to closely observe the customs of traditional Tibet. Along with a daily ritual of prayer and circumambulation, she had not worn secondhand clothes, she had not eaten food that was either too hot or too cold, too spicy or too sour. She had eaten mostly nourishing food and had taken care not to overeat. She had not drunk any strong liquors, nor large amounts of *chang*, the Tibetan barley beer. Once a month she had taken a little consecrated water, blessed by a spiritual master. She was also hoping to receive a long-life initiation from a high lama here in Dharamsala. That would be the highest blessing for the birth. Best of all, one night during her last month of pregnancy, she had had an auspicious dream, a rich, vibrant dream about a clear-eyed baby who seemed as if he or she would be familiar to Palmo in the future. Then the baby faded away before they could bond closely, although Palmo sensed the child would reappear when the time was right.

As she started down the path toward town and home, she detoured from the path to take a little side trail which took her into the woods. She walked slowly, enjoying being outside and alone. She knew this free time would disappear as soon as the baby arrived with all its demands for Palmo's energy and attention. The day was sunny and warm with a light breeze rippling only the uppermost branches of the encircling pine trees. After about half an hour her stomach started feeling very heavy. She hooked her hands under her ripened belly, using them to support its weight, and sighed. Her eyes were tired, and all the walking and standing up was getting much more tiring than it should. Her back, neck, thighs, and even her heart were beginning to ache.

As the aching intensified, she realized that the symptoms felt like the back labor pain. She quickened her step despite the contractions that were obviously gathering strength. She recognized the signs that the baby was finally getting ready to come out. She had known her time was getting near, but hadn't thought the birth was that imminent. She needed to get word to her husband, Ngawang, and the midwife Rinchen Lhamo.

As she neared home, her neighbor Sangmo leaned out from behind the curtain covering her front door and then quickly tied on her apron as she prepared to join Palmo. She had seen Palmo leave to walk to the temple and had roughly estimated how long she would be gone. In the past few days she had made it a habit of checking in every few hours when Ngawang was away just to make sure Palmo wasn't delivering alone. Just then Palmo's water broke, soaking her legs and feet and creating a big puddle on the path just outside the door to her house.

"Ah, now it is time to take you to the cleanest, quietest room of the house," Sangmo said with a laugh, as she took Palmo's elbow. Of course, there were only two rooms in the house and the one they had been preparing would only be partially quiet and clean. Sangmo sent one of her daughters to find Rinchen Lhamo to serve as midwife and another daughter to find Ngawang. Then Sangmo pulled a match out of the sash wrapped around her waist and lit the medicinal incense Ngawang had bought from the market a few days earlier. The incense was burnt to drive away bad spirits and to purify the house in preparation for delivery. And as the contractions gained strength, Sangmo and Palmo knew that the time for the baby's birth had come.

Tibetan Birthing

The fourth stage of the birthing process we have been following is the birth itself. Being born and giving birth are recognized as two of the major passages of life in virtually every culture. Both are profound, impressionable, deeply personal events. However, in the United States, giving birth often seems to be treated as a medical condition; in contrast, in the Tibetan tradition, giving birth is looked on as a very important, but entirely natural process. Perhaps it is due to this attitude—that birth is a natural process and not a medical condition—that for the vast majority of mothers the birth itself is fairly easy and straightforward. Of course, like anywhere, sometimes there are complications or deaths; but if the mother is healthy and the pregnancy has been normal, the birth predominantly goes well, especially if the woman is encouraged to follow her natural rhythms.

Tibetan culture prepares a woman for childbirth in many ways. First, a daughter learns all about the birth experience through her own mother's experiences during childbirth. As there are so many home births in Tibetan families, children will often wait nearby during the birth or will help out in some way with the delivery of their own brothers and sisters. Secondly, the Tibetan culture celebrates the entire birthing experience—preparations for labor, experiences during the delivery, and the time immediately after birth—with numerous rituals and traditions to mark the event.

In Dharamsala, I found that birth experiences varied from family to family. While many women follow the traditional practice and have their children at home, others will go to the Delek Hospital in Dharamsala or, for a more difficult birth, the more modern hospital in Kangra, an Indian town eleven miles away. I also spoke with Tibetan women who had their children in U.S. hospitals—an experience very different from the traditional Tibetan childbirth. In every experience, however, I found a common thread in the great sense of community support through the entire birthing process. Family and friends join together to comfort and nurture women giving birth and to welcome the precious new life of a child into the world.

It is also important to keep in mind that there are many customs and rituals in Tibetan culture before, during, and after birth—more than could possibly be represented in this book—and these customs vary according to geography, individual spiritual practices, and family traditions. For example, the people in Dharamsala, whose traditions play a primary role in this book, represent many regions of Tibet. Traditions will also vary according to the different sects of Tibetan Buddhism: Sakya, Nyingma, Gelugpa, and Kargyu.

Further, only a very small portion of the medical literature is dedicated to childbirth. Ngawang once pointed out to me that out of the five-year training at the Medical Institute in Dharamsala, only two or three days are spent on childbirth. This makes some sense, in that birth is such a natural part of Tibetan life that it wouldn't warrant a written record in a book. There is no lack of concern for women's health; it is simply usual to learn what is necessary through families and the community. However, the material that is included in traditional texts is studied with dedication and devotion. The Tibetans mix their own personal experience and knowledge of their culture with a familiarity with books and scholarly works—a rich and valuable mixture indeed.

Preparation for Birthing

In the Tibetan tradition, similar to the American custom, parents prepare for the baby's arrival beforehand; they make and purchase new items in preparation for the baby's homecoming. Even so, in Tibetan culture it is considered inauspicious to prepare too much beforehand—until they feel assured the baby will live. Sometimes new clothes and blankets are cut out, but they are not sewn together until after the birth. Of course, in most Tibetan cultures, friends, grandmothers, aunts, and even nieces or sisters, are available to make the new items immediately following the birth.

In the United States, people are often stressed by hectic schedules and do not usually have the support of large extended families nearby. Perhaps this accounts for some of the intensity of advance preparations for childbirth. Samten, a Tibetan woman raising her family in the United States, did her best to follow Tibetan tradition and made sure her baby's clothing was sewn by hand by a trusted family member who would put only loving thoughts into clothing that would touch, warm, and protect the newborn. This attitude is also common in the United States; "It was sewn with love" is a common expression that one hears when a friend or family member presents a blanket or clothes for a new baby.

"I made everything myself out of soft flannel," Samten told me. "Hat, pants, socks—I made it all by hand. If I had been in India or

Tibet, my family would have done this. Before my daughter was born, I made her a special Green Tara tanka. I bought a Green Tara tanka at the Tibet Shop in the city and then sewed the silk brocade around it. Usually this is done by specialized tailors, but since I was in the United States I had to do it myself. With the leftover material, I made my daughter a doll in the traditional Central Tibetan costume with jewelry. I made everything—the jewelry, the apron, and the shirt—so it will be special for her. We had a white scarf, the kata, on a small basket for her bed. A lama gave his blessing for Green Tara, so we consider Green Tara to be her goddess. And then Jetsun Kusho, a female lama in Vancouver, gave her the name Dolkar which is White Tara." (Jetsun Kusho is the sister of His Holiness Sakya Trizin, who is the head of the Sakya sect of Tibetan Buddhism. She one of the most highly qualified woman teachers in Tibetan Buddhism today and is a major holder of the Sakya lineage. It is considered an honor for one to have their child named by her.)

There are several Tibetan traditions designed to avoid negativity and "bad luck" prior to the birth. For instance, there is a traditional superstition that if a traveler, even a monk or nun, arrives at a house close to the time of birth, harm caused by bad spirits may later come to pass. To ward off such harm, prayers can be recited or certain rituals performed. In another birth superstition, five different colors of thread are traditionally threaded through a needle attached to the outside lintel of the door. This averts any danger. Alternately, a good luck swastika of barley flour is drawn on a piece of black material and shaken off outside. This, according to ancient belief, pacifies and drives away bad spirits. Today, however, traditional beliefs are not often given credence or practiced as fastidiously as they were in the past.

Before labor begins, blessed butter over which a mantra has been recited is prepared. A family member takes some butter to a lama and asks him to bless it. The lama holds the butter just under his chin, recites a mantra over it, and then blows on it; in this way the energy of the mantra is transferred into the butter. The butter is blessed well ahead of time and kept on hand for the birth, when it may be swallowed or rubbed on the body to ease labor, or used in rituals following the birth.

Birth Attendants

As the time of birth grows near, there is a sense of great expectancy and sharing within the entire family. Father, daughters, sons, and neighbors all get involved at one stage or another in helping during the birth. Everybody will help the mother to have as easy a birth as possible. It is traditional that the whole extended family should come together at this time and become involved as much as possible, with the women in the family usually playing the most central roles.

Even though the Tibetan people are well-known traders, and travel in yak caravans for hundreds of miles and months at a time across the Tibetan plateau and the Himalayas, it is considered important that a husband make every effort to be present at a birth. Arrangements to take care of all aspects of the birth are made throughout the extended family and community. Priority is given to the father's special place during the birth, to be present with the mother and any other children. His part in welcoming a child into the world is a sacred responsibility.

The sons do the external activities required, such as working in the kitchen, taking messages to people or relatives, arranging for the rituals and the rites, and inviting monks to say a special prayer. Sons generally stay in other rooms for the sake of privacy and do not usually come into the birthing room during the actual birth. Daughters, especially older daughters, are primarily responsible during the birth, staying with their mother or father and learning through the family and the neighboring midwife about the birth process that they will someday experience themselves.

The midwife or the father catches the baby (an amazing contrast to dominant American customs of recent decades, which prohibited fathers from even entering the delivery room until the 1970s, but have now changed to allow fathers work leave to enable them to be present at the birth and for family care). Normally a midwife supports the mother throughout the birth, assisted by all the family members. Some women work primarily as midwives, but in small villages that have low birth rates, women often can't sustain themselves as midwives. So these women might also work on a farm or find some other kind of work. When someone is giving birth, they are hired and given gifts in exchange for their services, although the gratuities are not usually in cash.

If there is no midwife, the mother, mother-in-law, father, daughters, or, in a well-to-do family, a close servant, may be the primary attendant. If there is no midwife or family member available, a woman gives birth by herself, as she has been taught to do since childhood. In a few parts of Tibet, custom has it that the father should not be anywhere near the birth. There is a saying that if he is present the baby may be too embarrassed to come out. That would delay the birth, especially if the baby is a boy. So in these areas of Tibet, the father must actually hide during the birth.

Despite the involvement of religious personages in every other aspect of the birth process—the many blessings and rituals—a monk would not be present during the actual birth. In the old tradition, delivery was seen as unclean and could be considered "polluting" to a monk.

Encouraging the Labor

In the Tibetan tradition, there are many rituals designed to bring on labor and to ease pain during labor. According to tradition, the ease of birth depends partly on the compatibility of the parents; if the parents are of similar stock, this usually indicates the child will be born without difficulty. For instance, as Palmo is short and slight and Ngawang is tall and broad-shouldered, Rinchen Lhamo surmised that Palmo might have difficulty if the baby has the build of Ngawang. It is believed, though, that children from parents of a "good stock" have supple bones, regardless of their size.

To ease and hasten delivery, there is an elaborate ritual in which a small piece of butter is molded into the shape of a fish with two eyes. A monk or respected family member recites a mantra over it two thousand times and blows the energy of the prayer into the butter. The butter fish is then given to the mother to swallow head first, without biting into it. (As described earlier, butter used in the birth is usually prepared beforehand.) Another traditional ritual involves a peacock feather and eight strands of hair from a bear, which are burnt together. The ashes are placed in a cup of water, and a mantra is repeated a hundred times.

It is believed that when the mother drinks this solution, she will give birth soon after.

A midwife may make a lemon herbal preparation, which the woman drinks as tea every fifteen minutes once labor begins. It works very well to help bring about an easy labor and birth.

As in most cultures, the first baby is generally considered to be the most difficult and is also considered to be an especially important child. In some parts of Tibet, there is a superstition that one should not give birth to the first child on the second or third floors. So people often give birth to the first baby in the basement. They say that with a first birth there is "so much pain the house could crack. The pain extends from all the mother's joints to her toes and she is numb all over."

A Traditional Birth: Palmo's Story Continued

Rinchen Lhamo walked briskly down the tree-lined path toward Palmo's house. A midwife for many years in Tibet, she only practiced occasionally now in Dharamsala. Still, her experience showed in her confident stride. Rinchen Lhamo was calm, peaceful, and fully alert with a clear look of purpose in her strong face. When she arrived, she found that Sangmo had persuaded Palmo to sip some strong broth to give her strength. Soon after, Palmo's husband, Ngawang, came running in the door.

"Is it time already?" he hurriedly asked of no one in particular. "Are you all right? Is the pain too much? Is it coming right now? Can I get you some food?" He asked a thousand questions of Palmo as he flung down his load and raced into the other room to collect blankets and pillows for her bed.

Ngawang would be present at the birth and help out when needed, though Rinchen Lhamo as midwife and Sangmo would do most of the work during the labor and birth. Laying out one of his ancient books, Ngawang began to recite a prayer specified to be recited during labor from one of the many volumes of the ancient *Collection of Mantras* (*gZungs bsDus*), a huge collection of ancient mantras, prayers, and praises to Buddha. Ngawang continued to periodically recite this labor prayer throughout the birth process.

Palmo was noticeably uncomfortable and a little irritable by this time. She had been in labor for a few hours now and it was past the time when she wanted to deliver. She alternated between lying down and pacing around the small house, sometimes sitting, sometimes squatting, sometimes on hands and knees, in her efforts to entice the baby to come out. Ngawang and Rinchen Lhamo talked briefly at the side of the main room, nodded together, and then Ngawang went to the kitchen area and brought out a square piece of butter. They decided to perform the rituals that are described in the medical scriptures to bring on birth when labor is long and difficult.

Ngawang made nine small indentations on the square of butter. Reciting the mantra OM SHA-SHA-LAM-PHYE SHU-SHU-LAM-PHYE two hundred times over the butter, he completed the empowerment of the butter by blowing over it. Then he went to feed it to Palmo. According to tradition, this would help Palmo give birth quickly. It is best if a Tantric practitioner does the recitation and ritual, but a doctor, uncle, father, or other person who has "kept his moral obligations" may do it.

"What has Palmo had to eat recently?" Ngawang asked. "Did she have any beer, garlic, or onions?" According to belief, such foods cause drowsiness due to their hot, acidic properties. They make the baby sluggish, weakening its ability to help in the birth process and so delay the contractions.

"She told me she hadn't eaten much," Rinchen Lhamo said. "She said she hadn't felt hungry all day. That blessed butter you just gave her should work though. It almost always does."

As if on cue, Palmo groaned loudly and got up from where she was lying on the bed. Sangmo and Rinchen Lhamo went to her sides, supporting her as she slowly walked around the room, moving her muscles one last time to help speed the birth.

Palmo stopped as a particularly strong contraction rippled through her. She squatted as blood and mucus were discharged. "That may be the baby turning, getting ready to come out head first," Rinchen Lhamo comforted her, as she massaged Palmo's legs and abdomen with sesame oil. Sangmo had two blankets over her arm, prepared to drape them over Palmo should she become cold at any point. Ngawang had just prepared a cup of warm butter tea to help speed the birth. He hastily put it on the table and rushed back to the kitchen to mix some warm melted butter. He gave this to Rinchen Lhamo to apply to Palmo's stomach to prevent the womb from being pushed out of place.

Palmo stood up again from her squatting position and slowly stumbled back to the bed. She sluggishly climbed on top of it and knelt on all fours as she started to push in earnest. Sangmo gently placed the warm blankets over her. "Don't push too hard," Rinchen Lhamo warned, wary of the danger of the womb collapsing. "Think of the sound of a tea brick being pounded in a mortar," she coached, "and push in that rhythm."

Concentrating on pushing in the tea-brick rhythm, Palmo sank into a kind of altered state, breathing heavily but regularly. The breaths and the rhythm seemed to smooth out in the final moments before the head suddenly appeared, a shiny black crown growing bigger and bigger. "One last push, one last push," Rinchen Lhamo said a couple of times, her hands gently catching the head, the tiny shoulders, then the back, and finally the whole baby in her palms.

Ready to rest, Palmo fell to one side as Ngawang and Sangmo caught her and laid her gently on her bed. Sangmo arranged more blankets around her. "The baby is here," Rinchen Lhamo whispered happily to Palmo, as she sprinkled a little cooling water onto her face to cleanse and refresh her. "Rest now, be happy. You have a healthy, beautiful baby boy."

Rinchen Lhamo carefully lifted the baby's legs so his head was lower down and cleaned his nose three times of mucus. With her finger she swept the tongue and inside of his mouth, again three times. Then she delicately placed the ring she had taken from Palmo's finger over the newborn's penis while Ngawang daubed the area with a symbolic smidgen of soot from the fire. "This will make sure he stays a boy and doesn't change into a girl!" Rinchen Lhamo said, laying the infant on his stomach at Palmo's side. With this movement the baby let out its first cry, a loud clear wail that seemed surprisingly strong, coming from such a small body.

Palmo propped herself up on her elbows, smiling broadly, the color quickly coming back to her strong face. Despite her fear of losing this baby, she reached out and laid an inquisitive hand on his head, then on his chest. Feeling such warmth and vitality inside his little body, she knew in her heart right then that he was healthy and strong and would take the place of the lifeless baby she had delivered last year.

Palmo lovingly cupped the baby to her side. Next to her, Ngawang greeted their new child with the auspicious words, "My child, you have been born from our hearts. May you live a hundred years and see a hundred autumns, may you have a long and glorious life, overcoming all ills and enjoying complete happiness, prosperity, and fortune." Ngawang looked intently at his new son as he offered this blessing, then lightly squeezed Palmo's hand.

Rinchen Lhamo carefully started to unwind the cord from around the baby's feet where it had tangled itself. She squeezed the blood in it with her fingers three times so the baby could benefit a last time from the rich nourishment of the placenta.

With Sangmo helping her, Rinchen Lhamo tightly tied a strong thread in a knot where the cord meets the navel and then another knot four finger widths up the cord from the first. Checking to make sure no blood was seeping, she poised the knife, and with one quick downward movement, cut the cord between the two knots. Ngawang mentally made note of the exact time the cord was cut so it could later be used in horoscopes. Ngawang had prepared some medicinal powder mixed with butter which he gave Rinchen Lhamo to apply to the navel. He would make sure that Palmo applied it daily thereafter until the healing was complete. When the cord fell off after a few days, Palmo would wrap it in a piece of cloth and pin it onto the shoulder of the baby's gown.

After the baby had rested on Palmo's stomach about fifteen minutes, Rinchen Lhamo, "a female helper blessed with good fortune" (as the medical text describes a suitable midwife) picked him up and bathed him in lukewarm water perfumed with Kashmiri saffron that Ngawang had bought for the occasion. The Kashmiri saffron would give the child a good complexion; the water for the bath, per tradition, was taken from a clean, running stream.

Immediately after the bath, Rinchen Lhamo and Sangmo wrapped the baby in soft, clean cloths permeated with the smoke of a specially-blessed incense that clears away evil forces. Rinchen Lhamo, "the helper with clean hands and well-cut nails," per the medical text and according to tradition, dipped a little cotton wool in oil and dabbed it on the baby's palate, providing him with healthy gums in the future. Before allowing the baby to suckle its first milk from Palmo, Ngawang opened the baby's mouth and drew the syllable DHIH on his tongue with saffron water, to give him the power of wise speech. They also looked to see if the baby was born with teeth and would watch carefully to see if the upper teeth grow first. Both occurrences are bad omens, foretelling some misfortune to the household. To avert this, fire offerings would be performed and offerings made to the deity Six-Faced Kumara (*Gzhon-nu gdong drug*). This baby, however, had only smooth gums with no sign of teeth, an auspicious sign, so these precautions were not necessary.

Rinchen Lhamo fed the baby a teaspoon of musk water that Ngawang had prepared earlier to protect the newborn from the earth gods who might want to reclaim him, and then gave him a mixture of butter and honey. As Palmo rose on one elbow to watch the administrations, Rinchen Lhamo placed the baby at Palmo's breast where he quickly learned to get his first meal. "Ah, see how strongly he sucks," said Ngawang proudly. "That is the sign of a healthy baby." In older times the baby would have waited two days to begin nursing. Butter from the female yak, or *dri*, would be given with a finger on the tongue until the post-colostrum milk came in. Nowadays parents understand the value of the first milk in providing healthy, natural immunization.

Sangmo had prepared a medicinal substance that was ground together and boiled in the milk of a white goat. She had sent her daughter to get the milk as soon as she heard Palmo was going into labor. This milk traditionally was brought by a girl coming from a direction south of the house, instructions Sangmo had hurriedly given her daughter as the girl ran to do her mother's bidding. According to legend, the girl should be from a good family and have both parents living, like Saraswati who was born in the southern ocean as the daughter of Brahma. This ritual would bring good fortune, and give the child wisdom, intelligence, a sweet voice, and a clear memory.[39]

Sangmo had been busy in the kitchen preparing meat broth, which she brought warm to Palmo to give her strength until the placenta came out. Palmo had held the newborn for a long time after the birth, then

Rinchen Lhamo came and took him in her arms and handed him to Ngawang to hold as Palmo prepared to discharge the placenta. The older children had been staying with a neighbor throughout the birth, though the oldest daughter, Khando, had come in every now and then to see if the baby had been born yet. At the moment of birth Ngawang had called all the children who were by that time hovering right outside the house. They came in to see their new brother with great curiosity and excitement. After eager questions and kisses to the new baby, they drifted off to play with the neighbors, the excitement over for the time being. Rinchen Lhamo had been pressing down on either side of Palmo's stomach with her hands, and soon the placenta slid out. Ngawang collected it in a bowl to save for burial a few days later.

Meanwhile Sangmo had prepared the traditional broth that is taken for strength and nourishment after the birth of the placenta. She had heated one-year-old rice wine, added boiled *tsampa*, and some dri butter. The one-year-old wine, it is said, helps to restore blood flow through the body, gives the mother fresh energy, and encourages rest. With all the care and attention directed toward her, the color was already returning to Palmo's skin.

After cleaning up, Rinchen Lhamo checked on Palmo to make sure everything was taken care of and made some soup and rice for Ngawang and Palmo to eat later on. Then, along with Sangmo, she said her good-byes and left Palmo to sleep and Ngawang to look after the baby. Sangmo would be back in an hour or two to help out with cooking, cleaning, and anything else that was needed. She was a good neighbor to them and would be the one to help out the most over the next few weeks.

Traditional Birth Rituals

Rituals are abundant during a birth, especially if the birth is a somewhat difficult one. If there is great difficulty during a delivery, a lama may be asked to do special prayers at the monastery that focus on childbirth. The father, or anyone else the family deems appropriate, approaches a rinpoche and makes an offering of a ceremonial scarf and some money in exchange for the appropriate ritual to be performed according to his divination.

Then the family member or friend goes to a monk or a monastery to have the ritual performed.

When a woman is in a very serious condition, her husband or other family members may do some divination with a lama. The divination is done through numbers, using something like dice. The lama shakes and throws the dice, and for each number there is a script, a bit like numerology. The lama throws a number of times and says many prayers so that the divination becomes proper and accurate. Then the lama tells what he sees and what will happen. When someone's life is at stake, the lamas do special life rituals.

In addition to blessed butter to ease especially strong labor pains, mothers may eat a certain dried fish from a sacred lake, especially Lake Manasarovar,[40] a holy lake in Tibet. This fish is considered an important item to help ease labor pains right before and during a birth. A little bit of the dried fish is kept on hand in most households and is fed to the mother when the pain increases. The piece of fish is believed to bring blessings and spiritual grace to the woman. Just a small bit eases the mind and helps the woman to relax, knowing she has received a blessing from the holy lake. Psychologically, just taking the butter or the fish makes the woman feel stronger. The belief in the blessing and feelings of support help her to stop worrying, and consequently makes the labor easier.

The modern mind may question the efficacy of all the Tibetan rituals and customs that take place during the birth process. Do they truly help the mother and child? One might assume that much of the aid is psychological, rather than spiritual or "mystical" in nature. In Jamyang Sakya's book *Princess in the Land of Snows*, when one of Jamyang Sakya's mother's closest friends was in labor, her mother went to her lama uncle to ask him to do prayers for her. He took the butter she had brought, blessed it, and put it in a container. She then ran back the two miles and gave her friend the butter. Then her friend had her baby so fast that they laughingly said the butter was still on the baby's head!

Rituals after Birth

According to ancient Tibetan traditions, there are several rituals that are often performed immediately following birth. These traditions may be found in the most ancient Tibetan texts and are pictured in the Illustrated Principles and Procedures. They are still upheld in many modern Tibetan families.

Immediately after the birth of a child, the mother is traditionally not supposed to touch any of the family property or, until it is washed, her hair. If she does, it is believed that whatever she touches will wear out or be lost quickly. To cleanse herself, the mother washes her face and hair in warm water and puts on clean clothes. Though birth is considered a natural and spiritual process, it is also in some ways considered unclean. Efforts are therefore made to purify the place and the people involved in the birth.

The birth position when the child is first born is considered very important, and this position is checked carefully for auspiciousness. It is auspicious if the head comes out first and the umbilical cord is wrapped around the upper parts of the body. And it is considered fortunate if the child cries out loudly when it is born. In the United States it is also considered a positive sign if the newborn lets out a good, healthy cry. In the Tibetan tradition, it is considered auspicious if the fontanel is a little elongated and soft, the forehead is a little small, and the hairline is very high. And it is good for the skin to have a good complexion and for the child to be able to suck strongly. All these characteristics are favorable and suggest that the child will be easy to raise.

In the same way, if a child has any features opposite to these, then it is not so auspicious and it is thought that this may be a difficult child to raise. Regardless of whether the child is born with these favorable features or not, as soon as a child is born, words of auspiciousness are recited. These words describe the qualities valued by the culture, such as being able to speak articulately, a lifetime of spiritual growth, and loyalty to one's family. These are recited in a ceremony of auspiciousness whether the child already has these qualities or not. In one version, the auspicious words are, "My child, you have been brought from my heart and from my stream of consciousness." Another is, "My son, it is as if you have been born from my mindstream. May you live for one hundred years. May you obtain great happiness and well-being. May you be free from the three poisons (of desire, hatred, and ignorance). And may you accumulate good merits and fortunes."

It is only after the recitation of these auspicious words that the umbilical cord is cut. To separate the umbilical cord, the midwife takes a piece of wool, rolls it into thread, ties the thread around the umbilical cord near the mother's body, and then cuts it off with scissors or a knife. Then the same procedure is performed to cut off the umbilical cord near the baby's navel. Soon after, the baby is placed near the mother's breast. After that, the parent or midwife takes certain herbs and roots, including blue gentian to prevent inflammation, mixes them with oil or butter, and applies the mixture to the navel. The baby is then washed with a soft cloth and warm water mixed with incense fluid or herbal fluid and wrapped tightly in cotton cloth and then wool for heat. It is significant that incense is used in the bath water, as incense is such an important part of every facet of Tibetan culture and permeates even cloth and buildings. Just as Tibetans offer incense to divine beings, with prayers, using the incense in the baby's bath represents the sacred nature of newborns and shows how human births are revered.

Immediately after the birth, saffron is stamped in the form of the syllable DHIH on the baby's tongue, in order to help the child sharpen his speech and memory. The DHIH is the seed syllable for Manjusri, the deity of wisdom, who is usually depicted holding a sword. As the sword symbolizes cutting through ignorance, parents symbolically bestow wisdom to their children when they stamp the syllable DHIH on the tongue. For Tibetans, marking the DHIH is the first step in developing the ability to speak articulately and to have clarity in communication, something that is tremendously valued in their culture.

In some parts of Tibet, a family member or midwife puts some blessed dri butter on the tip of the baby's nose. The butter is a symbol for nourishment and also symbolizes good health, longevity, and always having enough to eat. Then the blessed butter is also put on the child's tongue. This rich yak butter is a staple of the Tibetan diet. Root powder is mixed with butter and given to the child to strengthen the navel. The child's navel needs to be strengthened, as the navel area can easily become infected.

In order to ensure long life and health, musk is put in water, and the baby's right index finger is washed in that fluid. Then clarified butter or oil is placed on the navel, the ears, and the nose. Sesame oil or clarified butter are massaged into the head with cotton. The hand is considered too rough for the baby's skin, so the massage is done with cotton. A hat of cotton is made for the baby to wear. It is believed that this will help the child to be intelligent, have good blood flow in the brain, and grow into a bright and lively child.

To further increase intelligence, a small portion of *gassia* is given to the infant on his or her tongue. This is an herb to which musk, myrobalan fruit, cucumber seeds, and turmeric are added, along with honey or butter.

Babies are not held upside down by their feet, as one sees in many Western childbirth procedures. Tibetans believe that a newborn's internal organs are tender and soft, and do not want to do them harm. It is also considered very important that a baby stay with his or her mother. This concern for healthy "bonding" has become increasingly important in the United States as well.

Yeshe described the typical procedures following birth in their clinic at Tashi Jong. Interestingly, the afterbirth procedures in this more modern community clinic maintain many of the ritualistic traditions. "After the birth, we cut and tie the umbilical cord immediately and wrap the baby. The sister or father holds the baby. Then we wait ten to twenty minutes for the placenta. If it doesn't come, we hold the cord and slowly push down and pull. After the placenta comes out, we wash the baby. In some clinics the baby gets weighed right after birth too. If the placenta doesn't come in an hour and we think there is internal bleeding, we send the mother to the hospital a few towns over. That doesn't happen very often though. The placenta is buried in a deep hole dug in the ground. The umbilical cord is kept for about a year. The mother sometimes uses it to heal ash thrush, an occasional fungal growth in the baby's mouth. Dipping the cord in milk, tea, or water and rubbing it over the sore will bring healing."

According to other traditions, until the placenta is discharged, the mother should not take beer, curd, *lassi*, snuff, or tobacco, all of which produce heat in the stomach. But meat or tsampa broth, soup, or rice are recommended to give the mother back her strength. The mother may also drink one or two cups of hot butter tea. Sometimes a woman drinks a little alcohol after the birth to contract the uterus. In a very old tradition, they used to put the skin of a black snake over the mother's vagina for a short time to aid the mother's recuperation.

There is an old Tibetan custom (not much practiced anymore) to bring out the placenta. First, the cord is cut free from the baby. The end attached to the placenta is tied to a shoe, which provides a hanging weight. Then a basket, turned upside down, is placed on the floor. The woman walks around the basket clockwise three times, shoe dangling. She doesn't say anything while she goes around. And as she moves slowly, with a bit of swaying, gravity and movement help the placenta release. After that, the placenta is packed in a strong bag and buried deep in the earth, usually by the husband. It is buried deep because it is said that if a bird or animal happens to eat the placenta, the woman will become ill.

Tibetan Childbirth: The Modern Experience

A few hours away from Dharamsala is a health and birthing clinic in Tashi Jong (a community of about four hundred people). Yeshe, Dorje's mother and Lhamo's mother-in-law, lives half the year in a Tibetan community here and works as head nurse at the clinic. She regularly delivers babies for those who don't want to give birth at home. Increasingly, Tibetan women in Dharamsala are choosing to give birth in a hospital, in case of emergencies. But this choice depends on the personal situation of the mother. While insurance and monetary concerns are a factor in birthing decisions for U.S. mothers, the fee is very small in India and is not much of a factor in the decision of where a woman gives birth.

The clinic in Tashi Jong is small and centrally located, a five-minute walk from anywhere in the community. Yeshe described the clinic's part in the birth process: "When labor comes and the cervix is open, the mother calls us at the clinic, or has a grandmother come to let us know to expect her. When she comes, we check the blood pressure and pulse and wait usually seven to nine hours for the first baby. For other babies it usually only takes three to four hours. Sometimes the babies have large heads. In Tibet, the babies were never too big, so birth was easier. I think maybe that was because of the high altitude; less oxygen may affect the baby's size. Also we ate the foods in our environment." (It is interesting to note that in the United States we see lower birth weight in babies whose mothers smoke, which reduces the flow of oxygen to the fetus.)

Unlike the traditional Western methods, during a Tibetan birth at the clinic the mother is free to walk around, which often seems to hasten the delivery. Women may also choose the most comfortable position for the actual delivery. Many women choose to squat or kneel to give birth.

Yeshe and other medical technicians wash their hands before delivering a baby—one of the biggest changes Tibetans have made in their childbirth practices. Since it was often so cold in Tibet, washing came to hold little value in Tibetan culture, even during birth. A Tibetan doctor in the United States told me that infection, due to lack of a clean environment, coupled with the lack of understanding of infection in Tibetan medicine, was one of the greatest causes of infant mortality there.

Yeshe produced some impressive statistics from her seventeen years at the clinic. "Since 1972, only two children have been stillborn," Yeshe told me. "If there is any difficulty at birth, we have special rituals done for the safety and health of the mother and baby." While it's difficult to say whether these outcomes are a result of the services by the community clinic, five observations seem significant: the clinic is accessible and convenient; it is familiar with the health needs of the families it serves; the staff is part of the community and so knows those who come and is trusted by them; and the birth time is relatively short before the family walks home with their newborn. And, as in all Tibetan medicine, the relationship between helper and family is sacred.

Many women opt to have their babies in the Delek Hospital in Dharamsala, the local hospital, which offers some Western allopathic services and also Tibetan ways of care. But facilities here are very limited. For difficult births, women are taken to Kangra Hospital, the Indian hospital in Kangra, about eleven miles away. Making the decision to go to a hospital at a distance is difficult. Often it is hard to find someone with a car, and a taxi is expensive. Also the roads are in bad shape, so the ride itself may be quite difficult for the patient. And once at the Kangra Hospital, which has an Indian staff, many Tibetans say that they do not receive the same treatment as they would at the local hospital, with Tibetan care from those they know. They may miss their family support, the sense of the sacred, and feel as strangers in another community.

Labor

It is during the labor itself that Tibetan traditions seem to differ the most from the usual Western techniques. Several Tibetan women who had experienced labor in the United States told of their experiences. While they understood that sterile conditions may benefit both mother and child, especially in a hospital setting (in good health, people accommodate to and develop an immunity to germs they live with), they sensed the loss of a great deal of warmth, both literally and psychologically.

Jamyang Sakya has experienced childbirth in both Tibet and the United States and, in 1961, was the first Tibetan refugee to give birth in the United States. She spoke about the differences between having her babies in the United States and in Tibet. "It was very, very different," she said, quickly and definitely. "In Tibet we take care of the baby but we also do lots of things for the mother's health. We clean her, give her hot melted butter to help heal her, and generally take special care of her. But in the United States, the mother just lays on her side and they give her cold water."

Samten has only experienced birth in the United States but grew up with Tibetan customs: "My mother gave birth to nine children, all in our home, so I had seen what childbirth was like and was prepared to do my best. Even with that preparation, my baby was so large that I had to take a C-section. So I was glad to give birth in a hospital; the techniques in the United States are very good." Still, like Jamyang Sakya, she was surprised by the differences in procedures. "It was too cold. In the Tibetan tradition, we always keep warm, especially while having a baby. My mother kept my sisters warm when they had their babies and gave them chicken soup. My husband brought me some chicken soup, but the hospital said I was not allowed to eat it. I told the nurses I was cold and thirsty and they gave me ice cubes!"

In the Tibetan tradition, women are always kept warm during labor. It is believed that a woman uses the energy of her whole system in pushing the baby down, and consequently becomes cold. To keep warm, she must have something warm to eat, a hot meal. As a woman's teeth are very loose at this time (according to folk belief, all the ligaments and bones are more flexible for birth) she isn't given anything to chew. But she is given warm liquids for a couple of days, and delicate foods like porridge, chicken soup, or tsampa soup.

In the United States, a mother is given a careful medical exam after delivery and then put in a room to rest. In contrast, in the Tibetan tradition they feed a mother lots of food after she gives birth—as with Palmo's birth, in which the kitchen was constantly active with the preparation of all sorts of hot foods for her. In Tibetan culture, conventional wisdom usually helps ease the situation. In a classic clash of "East meets West," Samten and many other Tibetans experiencing U.S. childbirth procedures have never even had ice water before. Tibetans generally don't drink cold water—just tea, chang, whey, buttermilk, milk, and sometimes hot water. In fact, in some areas it is considered an insult to offer a visitor cold water to drink.

While many Tibetans enjoy living in the United States and appreciate the hospital system with all its available technology, the experience in a hospital, with all its rules and regulations, can be an ordeal. Of course, this is true for many American mothers as well, but it is especially hard for women who come from such a different tradition. Certainly, modern practices have much to offer in sanitary conditions and medical expertise during difficult births (caesarean sections, and so forth), but many mothers, both American and Tibetan, talk about the human factor getting lost amid all the technology.

Infant Mortality

According to Dr. Lobsang Rapgay, in Tibet many families have one or more children who die as babies, and the dead child is usually replaced with a newborn child, much as Palmo replaced her loss with a new baby. In Tibet, there has been and continues to be a high rate of infant mortality, both soon after birth and up to a couple of years after birth. Under Chinese occupation, poverty and malnutrition make pregnancy more difficult.

Many children die prematurely. One Tibetan scholar told me that Tibetans believe very strongly in karma and do not take health conditions into consideration at all. Dr. Rapgay said, "It's so cold that Tibetans in many villages don't bathe for months. Sometimes it's just once a year, in the summer. Sanitation is not economically or socially of value."

Dr. Rapgay says that in India, he hears of fewer and fewer cases of Tibetan babies dying: "Nearly everybody seems to be delivering well and healthily now. But it was not so in Tibet. My mother gave birth to fifteen children. Only nine survived. That ratio was quite common. It looks to me as if many Tibetan children died because of an infection that set in. Both the Tibetan doctor and certainly the family would not be able to recognize it as an infection. The death would frequently be sudden. Often the death would be attributed to some spirit, but it was more likely lack of basic sanitation."

It's very difficult to understand how a parent could lose so many children and still carry on. But the Tibetans often view this tragic event as they do all other aspects of the birth process—as a natural process.

Palmo had lost a baby the year before. "It arrived two weeks early," she told me. "At eight-and-a-half months pregnant. I just started bleeding—with no signs, no pain, nothing. My husband and a neighbor took me to Delek Hospital in Dharamsala. At that time the fetal heart beat was okay and I could feel the baby moving. But our hospital has very limited facilities, so I went down to Kangra Hospital. Then, on the way, the pain started. I nearly died then. And then, when I reached Kangra, I waited for over an hour for the doctor to come and see me. By that time, the doctor said the fetal heart was not heard, and the baby was dead.

"In medical terms, they say the placenta was blocking the birth channel," Palmo elaborated, giving the medical reason for the death of her baby. "Usually it's the head first, and then soon after the baby the placenta follows. But sometimes the placenta moves before the head, and it blocks the route. The baby has to push through and the placenta ruptures. That is where the blood comes from. Then the baby suffocates and dies. I think it's something like that."

There were a lot of rituals to be done, including the life rituals for Palmo as her condition was critical. "Ngawang wonders if maybe I lost my child because I ate meat from a neighbor who doesn't have children. Not because of the meat itself, but because she had given me the meat. No matter what it was she gave me, whether it's meat or another food, it would have caused trouble."

Other preparations include different ways of avoiding negativity or *dip*, the invisible pollution or negative essence associated with something that may be intangibly harmful, such as eating food prepared by women who are barren. In Tibetan culture, folklore suggests that a woman who cannot have children of her own may unconsciously cause harm to a pregnant woman. Sometimes this is described as witchcraft. It is believed that negative energy is passed to the pregnant woman, and food is the vehicle through which this negativity is most often carried. For this reason it is customary that pregnant women do not accept food from anyone except immediate family members.

A Tibetan friend in Dharamsala and a Tibetologist in California both observed that Tibetan witchlore is as disturbingly misogynist as witchlore in many other cultures and does women much more harm than good. Childrearing has been and continues to be a praiseworthy and highly valued activity in Tibetan society. Tibetans in exile are having far fewer children than they would have had in Tibet, but having babies is expected of women, unless they are nuns. Women who are not nuns and do not have or want children occasionally feel some prejudice in Tibetan culture, though few people say anything directly.

"But the baby should not have been the victim," Palmo continued, searching for a meaning to comprehend why this happened to her when she was so healthy throughout the pregnancy. "Why did it have to happen? It's hard to understand." Palmo looked at her hands in her lap, caught between searching for an explanation and just accepting, for whatever reason, that it happened. "Whatever happens has to have a cause. You can't have an experience without an explanation. The deity or whatever it was, positioned the placenta that way. I would have had an operation if it would have saved the baby. But the doctor said that it was no use because I had lost a lot of blood." Palmo looked directly at me, her eyes strong and tender. "After a week when I was able to move around, I came back to Delek Hospital and got two units of blood. Actually I needed more, but I didn't want to bother people. But I'm okay now." She smiled and lightly shrugged her shoulders, indicating that what's past is past, a common attitude among Tibetans.

Even though Palmo's experience was very traumatic, she did not dwell on her personal loss, but emphasized the intricate pattern of life and death. In addition, she was genuinely interested in examining both the medical and traditional causes for the placenta being in front of the baby rather than in its normal place. She was able to integrate both explanations. The diagnosis that the placenta was in front of the baby and that its rupture caused the severe bleeding, answered her question of what happened physically. But she still wanted to know more, such as why it happened at all, and found that the traditional Tibetan beliefs provided an explanation that substantiated her experience. Perhaps living in Dharamsala, with its greater influence of Western philosophy and science, contributed to Palmo's integration of both explanations. Perhaps such communities can assist the rest of the world to integrate differing cultures.

Like Palmo, many Tibetan families who lose infants want an explanation of not only what happened, but why. The concept of infection satisfies their desire to know the medical cause of their baby's death, but many Tibetans also want to know why the infection set in. Why, even though sanitation is poor all over Tibet, do some babies die from infection or disease, and others live?

In Western medical practice it is known that a baby is susceptible to infection when unsanitary conditions are present. In Tibetan tradition, though, it is believed that spirits, deities, witches, barren women, and the like, cause a particular person, or baby, to be overtaken by infection or illness—which explains why others in the same physical environment are not affected at all. In Western medicine, research findings are helping us accept the influence of emotions, thoughts, laughter, visualization, and spiritual faith in the healing process.

"When the cause can be attributed to spirits and other things," Dr. Rapgay explained, concentrating on the psychological benefits of finding explanations for death and illness, "it is less upsetting than not knowing, because understanding the cause is a strong Tibetan value.

When misfortune can be accepted as part of the process of life and death, it's much easier."

In one meeting with Dr. Rapgay, I asked him about the medical analysis of a traditional Tibetan birth, looked at from both his perspective as a doctor in training in Dharamsala and from his knowledge of the Western medical system. He explained soberly, "In Tibet, when the cord was cut, the room might have been very dirty; there was no way to sanitize it. Very minor things which are taken for granted both in the United States and in Delek Hospital explain why so many babies in Tibet died. The births were always at home. The medical institutions had no facilities for delivery.

"Tibetan medicine is good for many health concerns, but has very little infectious disease control. Our country is so cold, it deadens many viruses. The Tibetan system works on the body as a whole, not on specific problems. Tibetan medicine is not designed to treat a heart problem. It is designed to show how heart disease might affect the whole body, and to bring the whole system into balance. So Tibetan medicine is most effective with many of the systemic illnesses that are more difficult to treat with the Western medical system, while Western medicine works effectively with health issues not addressed in Tibet.

"In the childbirth procedures in Tibet, people were on their own to determine if what they were doing was right or wrong. There was no governmental system to tell them that for a child to be born safely certain basic requirements had to be met. The people had to make their own choices."

Analyzing these different birth stories shows us how something as natural and universal as birth can have so many different variations amongst different cultures, as well as individuals. Each of the Tibetan women who had recently given birth—Palmo, Lhamo, and Tsering—had different experiences. Their babies had made their individual marks simply through the way they entered the world and met their families and surroundings.

Today, Tibetan women and families in much of the world have an increasing degree of choice in how and where they will have their babies. Whether they choose a traditional method, modern birth in a hospital, or another alternative, whatever the religious affiliations, homeland, or family traditions, may they find the path that fulfills their needs and the destiny of a precious new life.

Young Tibetan father with the family's newest member.

5:   Bonding

Gems of Tibetan Wisdom for Bonding

◊   *Bonding begins during preconception and in the womb and develops through the love, closeness, and depth of relationship that grows between parents and child.*

◊   *There is a time for family bonding and cleansing after birth and before the celebration in which the community welcomes a new baby.*

◊   *Continuous bodily contact with mother, father, and other members of family and community is assumed to be natural and essential for the development of the brain.*

◊   *Nursing should begin soon after birth, and the mother needs to be aware that she feeds her feelings to her baby through her milk; the mother needs to deal with any feelings of anger, greed, or denial so they do not poison her child.*

◊   *Water, sun, touch, fresh air, and massage also provide the baby with needed nourishment and connection to the earth.*

◊   *Naming is a way to bond the baby to its spiritual heritage; names are often given by a lama or the Dalai Lama; the day of the week on which a child was born may also be given as a name.*

◊   *Tibetan medicine acknowledges and understands postpartum depression and its treatment and thus how to improve mother-infant and family relationships at this crucial time.*

Dolma Tsering: A Family United

Quietly, and unbeknownst to everyone but close members of their family, Dorje bundled his new daughter in layers of warm blankets, placed her in Lhamo's arms, and asked Yeshe, the grandmother, to stay with them as he found a taxi to drive them all home from Delek Hospital. While the family's birth experience reflected Dorje and Lhamo's Western lifestyle, they did not want to take the chance of bringing bad luck by talking about it too much and didn't mention to anyone they passed along the way that they were carrying a newborn infant in their bundle. Word would leak out soon enough, and family and friends would come to the customary community welcoming ceremony following a quiet time for family transition, bonding, and cleansing rituals.

When Lhamo and Dorje walked in the door of their house with their new daughter, a great commotion greeted them. Their two sons, Tenzin and Gyamo, began running all around the room in their excitement. One of Lhamo's close friends had stayed with them while their parents were at the hospital. Tenzin was eager to meet his new sister. "Let me see, let me see," he said as he pulled at Lhamo's arm, stood on his tiptoes, and peered into the bundle that she lowered for him to see.

Lhamo told him he could look at his sister but couldn't touch. "She's so tiny that you must be careful with her," she warned. Dorje also warned them to be gentle, knowing that in their excitement to see their new sister they might accidentally hurt her. The warnings did little good, though, as the boys crowded close and smothered her face with kisses in their enthusiasm. The baby sputtered from all the attention, but didn't cry, her parents noticed happily.

The next morning, sure enough, word had spread to friends and family, and Dorje received congratulations from a well-wishing neighbor. "The baby was born last night. Come visit in three days time," Dorje replied, his voice sounding a bit tired but obviously relieved. "Don't come before that though. We won't let you in any earlier." He laughed at this direct reminder of his culture's traditions, and added, "It's a girl."

For the next few days, the baby settled in with her family. Lhamo settled on a bed in the main room, which would serve as a focal point for the activities of the house during the day. Here, Lhamo could easily pick up, nurse, and play with her new daughter. The baby lay next to her, sleeping when she liked. Dorje was busy helping with all the extra chores that needed to be done: watching the other children, washing diapers, and making special meat broth, chicken soup, tsampa, and butter tea for Lhamo. He also had to heat water for Lhamo, as, per tradition, she was not allowed to touch cold water for the first month after birth. Doing so, it was thought, might give her back problems in the future.

According to custom, Dorje went to a high lama two days after his daughter's birth to receive a name for her. As was usually the case, the lama he visited was one who was regularly consulted by the family for ceremonies and special needs. Dorje prostrated himself and made a small offering of money. He also brought a ceremonial scarf which the lama blessed and returned to him, placing it gently around his bowed neck.

"Is the baby a boy or a girl?" the lama asked.

"A girl," Dorje answered proudly. The lama, sitting upright, concentrated his full energies on the new baby. After a few minutes he raised his cupped hands to his mouth and blew his blessing on the colorful silk knotted protection cord they held. Handing the cord to Dorje, and at the same time naming the infant, he said, "This is for your daughter, Dolma Tsering."

Dorje bowed respectfully to the lama, accepted the protection cord to pin on his daughter's shirt, and hurried home with the blessed string. He was excited to tell Lhamo the special name their daughter had received, for the validation of her name gave the newborn another stronghold on the life she was just beginning.

Dolma Tsering's birth, as was the custom in their village, would be celebrated with purification and welcoming ceremonies on the fourth day after the actual event. Lhamo, Dorje, and Dorje's mother, Yeshe, began the day of rituals with the contemplation of the deities and protectors. Then Dorje went to see the lama who named his daughter to have a special bottle of water blessed to be ready for the day's rituals.

When he returned, they performed the cleansing ceremony. Dorje poured some of the holy water into Yeshe's cupped hands, and she added her blessing to the water. Then Yeshe poured some of the twice-blessed water into Lhamo's palm. Lhamo drank a little and then wiped her palm on her own head and on Dolma Tsering's small head. That completed the cleansing of any impurities associated with the birth. And it also bound Dolma Tsering more deeply to the traditional ways.

The Welcoming Ceremony

While Dolma Tsering's family enacted these rituals, visitors prepared for the fourth-day welcoming party. And by the time Dorje's brother, Dhonden, and his wife, Lhakpa Dolkar, walked up to the doorway, the family was ready to greet them.

"We have come to welcome the new baby," Lhakpa Dolkar said, presenting a kata, a white blessing scarf, to Dolma Tsering, who lay peering up out of Lhamo's lap.

As the first visitor's arrival marked the end of the family time alone, Dorje prepared incense and a small container of milk. Giving a small prayer for Dolma Tsering, Dhonden lit the incense and sprinkled milk around the room, thereby cleansing the house and inaugurating Dolma Tsering's welcoming ceremony.

Dorje brought auspicious tea and rice from the kitchen which he gave to everyone present and to other guests as they arrived. Some of them had brought presents: a small bag of tsampa (barley flour), a cake of butter, tea, *chang*, baby clothes. Dorje's sister Choeling brought a small, handmade cloth doll to her new niece. Dorje received the gifts on Dolma Tsering's behalf.

Friends and relatives dropped in throughout the festive day, bringing small presents and good wishes for Dolma Tsering to celebrate her arrival into both the family and the community. Filled thermoses of butter tea were poured, and trays of freshly fried Tibetan cookies were passed around. After a while, Dorje brought out dishes of rice mixed with raisins and butter. Each guest came to take a handful, some to eat and some to throw into the sky, for the child's auspicious life. The rice symbolized both protection for the young baby and the harvest of nine months of pregnancy. Dolma Tsering spent the day on Lhamo's lap. The visitors respected the Tibetan tradition in which people outside of the immediate family do not touch newborns right away, usually waiting until the child is a month or so old and is strong enough not to pick up any illnesses from adults through the contact. Many of the guests stayed late into the evening enjoying a dinner of hearty *thugpa* soup and drinking glasses of chang, the local Tibetan barley beer.

Though she slept for some of the time, Dolma Tsering had spent this day among the people with whom she would be closest as the years went on. This special meeting established her relationship with them and her right to receive their care and love as long as they live. It also cemented her responsibility to care for and love all of them as she grew older.

Bonding in the Tibetan Tradition

In every tradition, the time immediately after a birth is considered special and important as it is the time of bonding between child and parents. In the Tibetan tradition, the strands that affect the quality of bonding between parent and child are knit together especially at this time, as well as throughout their relationship. Bonding begins as early as conception (or even before conception, through life after life) and strengthens as the pregnancy progresses. With the birth and the care of an infant after birth, bonding takes on new and deeper dimensions. From the moment the mother and father first hold their baby and throughout the early caretaking process, the bond between them intensifies. When the family moves as a unit for the first time, such as an outing on an auspicious day, it is considered an especially significant time in the initial postbirth bonding. Especially in the first few days of newness and transition, when a child is being assimilated into the family, a family is in a state of heightened awareness.

According to Tibetan custom, the family spends several days alone immediately following birth. Families usually welcome these traditional days of quiet and use this time to get used to the demands of a new infant and to enact rituals and prayers for the newborn. During this time, families rarely go out and visitors know that they must wait for the customary few days of family time (three days for a boy and four days for a girl) before they formally recognize the birth and welcome the new baby into the community. The number of elapsed days before visitors are allowed to see the baby is the only difference between celebrating the birth of a boy and the birth of a girl. In the traditional view, visiting any earlier than three or four days may bring bad luck for the child or the parents and could cause the baby to lose its tenuous hold on life. In some traditions, the house of a newborn is regarded as polluted, so people stay away until the third or fourth day after delivery when the family has completed the cleansing rituals.

The purification ceremony, called *Bang-so*, is done in the morning on the third or fourth day. This short religious ceremony involves the burning of purifying incense, the common Tibetan method of cleansing invisible dirt. Then neighbors, friends, and relatives arrive with presents for the welcoming ceremony to celebrate the birth. The visitors usually bring small gifts for the child. And if the child has a nanny or nurse, as was common with upper-class families in Tibet, a packet of money and a ceremonial scarf would be given to this caregiver as well.

However, not all visitors are welcome. Tradition bars married women who have been unable to have children of their own from interacting with newborns. "Excuses are made," a Tibetan mother explained to me, "so that a barren woman is not allowed to hold or see a newborn—which is difficult because a relative is socially expected to greet a child. But the woman's barrenness is considered suspect. It is not a subject Tibetans usually talk about, but when a woman does not visit to welcome a new child, it implies that she is barren and knows that she is not welcome." While many Tibetans who analyze this situation believe that this cultural superstition is hurtful and wrongfully biased against women without children, this attitude still runs deep throughout Tibet. In Western societies, in which increasing numbers of women are not having children or are having children at much later ages, the superstition is likely to change sooner.

In the Tibetan tradition, a newborn will not be taken out of the house for several weeks. In some Tibetan practices, the child is taken out of the house for a short outing either three days after a child is born or on an auspicious day. This ceremony is called *Go-don* which means "exit." After this, the child is not taken out again for at least a month. In some parts of Tibet, a child is secluded at home for six or seven months to protect him or her from harm, a custom which may have had its origins in the rigors of an extreme climate. This tradition is no longer practical in modern times and has fallen out of general practice. Traditionally, the first time a baby leaves the house, an astrologer is consulted to confirm an auspicious day for such an undertaking. When the baby arrives at a friend's house on one of these short outings, the friend places a kata or a little butter on its head. They may also give a little tsampa or small gift to celebrate the visit of the new baby.

Breastfeeding and First Foods

Breastfeeding is considered to be a very important contributor to the child's health and general welfare. As discussed in earlier chapters, Tibetan women are usually very careful to follow good nutrition during pregnancy and through the infancy and nursing period in order to provide the best health for the baby. This ideal is held in both Eastern and Western traditions—an increasing number of women in the United States also stop drinking alcohol, smoking, and watch their diet when they are pregnant and nursing.[41] Indeed, women throughout the world are becoming more concerned with nutritional concerns to safeguard the health of the newborn.

In the Tibetan tradition, women normally breastfeed their children for years after birth. As mentioned in the chapter on birthing, one positive influence by modern medicine is that Tibetan women now usually feed their infants the first milk, the colostrum, as they have heard from Westerners and others that it is healthy. Traditionally, the colostrum was thrown away in the belief that it was impure.

If a woman is unable to nurse or her milk is considered unhealthful for some reason, another woman may be selected to nurse the child. However, because this is such an important event, the family confirms beforehand that the other woman is goodhearted, free from illness, from a good family, and has a special quality that fits in with the child's personality. In an interview, the Dalai Lama said that a mother has direct influence on her child's mind, beginning before birth, continuing through her milk, and on into the relationship that grows between them. The

Dalai Lama clearly showed a parallel between the mother's influence on a child's consciousness and nursing—a physical bond in which the mother's essence literally pours into the child. Characteristically, he integrated the physical and the spiritual realms naturally and without emphasizing the importance of one over the other.

While mother's milk is the main nourishment for the growing baby, this diet is soon supplemented with tsampa, the roasted barley flour that is the staple of the Tibetan diet. Tsampa is prepared and eaten in many forms. It is often the main item of every meal and may also be eaten both as a snack and mixed into tea and beer. Eating tsampa is one of the most universal elements of the Tibetan people's life and culture. Eager to incorporate a baby into his or her heritage and expected lifestyle, parents often feed their child a thick paste of tsampa, boiled water, and butter, in tiny portions the size of the tip of the little finger, as early as a day or two after birth. Tsampa, in addition to providing nourishment, serves to draw the baby into the heart of a central nurturing activity of the family and of Tibetan culture.

Just as tsampa helps to make the baby strong physically and culturally, it is believed that placing a dab of butter on the soft spot on top of the baby's head for the first seven to ten days of his or her life will make the baby strong bodily and spiritually. Like tsampa, butter was, and continues to be, a staple of the Tibetan diet; using it daily on the newborn serves to bond the baby to the fabric of the culture—a fabric that the baby is woven into with each new ritual and custom.

Sex Change

In Tibetan culture, the folklore belief is that a baby's sex can change either during pregnancy, right at the moment of birth, or up to a few days after birth. Changing sex is not seen as bad, but is to be avoided since it is unsettling to the child and family and is considered different from the way things were originally meant to be. A doctor at the Tibetan Medical Institute estimated that perhaps one in one hundred babies change their sex. Tibetans from all socioeconomic levels consider it a fairly common occurrence. Tibetan people in Dharamsala mentioned naturally that some babies change their sex. Just as Ngawang and Palmo placed a gold ring on their newborn son's penis for the first few days to keep him from changing sex, most people I talked to said that sex change does indeed happen and that it is somewhat common.

However, the sentiment "I've heard about sex change many times, so maybe it's true. But I haven't seen it" was one I often heard from people. They all agreed that sex change happens, is not really rare, and is certainly possible. But no one I talked to had seen it, though many knew of others who said their baby changed sex. So while in Western cultures the sex of the baby is one of the most definite pronouncements made immediately after the birth—"It's a girl!" can be heard ringing forth loud and clear as soon as the baby emerges—in the Tibetan culture the gender of the baby is seen as much more transitory, able to shift throughout the pregnancy and for the first few days after birth.

Tibetan parents will sometimes say a baby is a girl—even if the child is very obviously born a boy. This is supposed to prevent a sex change from happening and keeps the spirits or human curses from bringing harm or illness to the baby. They will also change a name during childhood to fool evil spirits. I spoke to one woman who said she believed that she did not reach puberty until the very late age of eighteen because she was originally a boy and her body became confused. It is often said that young girls who are tomboys were originally born as boys.

Although attitudes have changed somewhat, Tibetans generally prefer the first child to be a girl so that when she grows up, she will be more useful to the family. In addition it is believed that when the first child is a girl her parents are ensured a long life. Often a girl is preferred because no monks will come to take her away for teachings at the monastery. On the other hand, a monk told me that boys are preferred in Tibetan families. From other Tibetans, I've been told that each gender is valued equally. The monk may have been thinking about all the good work boys can do in the monastery and was therefore more inclined to value boys. But overall, the choice of a boy or a girl seems to be more a personal preference that varies from family to family.

The prevalent belief that barren women may, either consciously or unconsciously, pass some of their "witchcraft" through food to pregnant women applies also to the changing of sex. I heard a number of stories from women who believed they had given birth to a child of one sex, who then turned out to be the other. Nearly all said they had been pressured into accepting food from barren women when they should not have eaten with them because of the perceived risk to their babies. To avoid such misfortunes, the mother is encouraged to avoid quarreling with other women and is told that she should not visit barren women's houses or eat anything given to her by a barren woman. As a further precaution, she should touch the baby's genitals or put a gold ring on a male child's penis immediately after he is born.

Rituals During the Bonding Period: Celebration and Cleansing

Once I asked Tashi why there were so many rites and rituals surrounding the birth of a child. He replied, "The threats to a child's survival in the austere climate of Tibet are so real, so constantly ever-present, that rites and rituals assume great importance. In modern society those threats are relatively nonexistent, so rites and rituals do not have the same meaning." These rites were originally designed, in their way, to tie a newborn to life itself. In the modern Tibetan tradition, these rituals still play a profound role in bonding a Tibetan child to family and culture, a spiritual heritage, and to the cycles of life and nature.

The rituals performed during the days after birth particularly mark a newborn's integration into this world and begin to carve a niche in the patterns of relationships the child will have both with family and the deities. Offerings are made to the deities and protectors, butter lamps are lit, and prayers may be chanted in the house to honor the new baby. On the day visitors are expected to come, as described earlier, full rituals and prayers are given on the child's behalf. Grandparents also help prepare for the birth and the surrounding rituals, both spiritually and physically, as Yeshe did for Lhamo and Dorje.

Not long after birth, families perform a few small rituals to empower the child and to ensure good health. As in other traditions, there are whole groups of rituals for different spiritual practices. The specific characteristics of the ceremonies may also depend on a lama's divinations and different family traditions. The rituals can be done by the family or a few monks at the child's home, or by many monks at the monastery. Gyatso once told me, "If the family sees that the child has some beauty of character or some dynamic energy, they will consider the child spiritually important. To express this special feeling about the child, they will do extra rituals until other people also become conscious of the child as someone special."

Very often, this recognition of spiritual importance means that the child could be a reincarnate of an honored spiritual or learned teacher, or that he or she has enormous capacities for growth, helping others, or becoming a spiritual teacher. To ensure that a child's capacities have a greater chance of developing, elaborate rituals are performed to protect a new child and to facilitate spiritual growth. Although it is possible for any child to be the reincarnate of a great lama or teacher, most families think of this potential in the abstract while they treat their child as an ordinary baby, unless the infant gives signs of having a special gift. For instance, Lhamo and Dorje consider their newborn daughter special to them, but do not treat her as anyone holier than a much-loved new addition to their family.

Rituals may be done to protect newborns and older children from the influence of human curses and evil spirits through the years of early childhood. For instance, in one ritual a child is fumigated with a smelly concoction of betel nut, cashew, and turmeric to help scare away any unknown spirits. Then a special threaded charm, which contains cashew root, is tied around the neck or each wrist of the infant to protect him or her from evil spirits. According to tradition, some people even tie the charm around the crown of the child's head. At least once every month, parents protect the child further with special rites and rituals conducted to pacify the spirits. The child does not actually need to be present at these ceremonies; they can be done on his or her behalf by a family member.

In another cleansing method, which is sometimes used to remove illnesses, tsampa dough or wheat flour is given to the mother and then to the baby. The dough is rolled all over the child's body to pick up the negativities and toxicity from the birth, and then the baby squeezes it in his or her two fists. That impression is then taken and cast away with effigies that have been made from dough by a lama in the likeness of the intruding spirits. This ritual is also performed when there is any sort of danger present to the child's well-being, such as high fever, repeated nightmares, unexplained fears, or fits of crying. According to tradition, the barley flour dough becomes food for the effigy so that the offending spirit will feel that it has had enough to eat and will not be interested in bothering the baby further.

After the umbilical cord falls off, it is usually preserved and kept in a safe place for later use when the baby has a cold sore, rough tongue, or fungal infection. At that time it is dipped in water, honey, or sometimes butter and rubbed on the sore as a cure. Traditionally, the cord is considered an important medicine for infants. Sometimes it is boiled in water, and the soup from it is fed to the baby. Additionally, it can be tied into an amulet and worn around the infant's neck. The use of the baby's own umbilical cord for healing symbolizes a powerful sense of connection and continuation through the gestation, birth, and infancy of the child.

Dorje: Burial of the Placenta

After Dolma Tsering's birth, the placenta, which had been her home within her mother, had been carefully wrapped. One sunny day, during those first quiet days at home, Dorje invited his older children, Dolma Tsering's brothers, to join him on a walk. "Today we are going on a special outing," he told them. "We shall go together and bury the placenta of the new baby in a safe place deep in the earth way up in the woods in the mountain. Who will join me?"

"I will, I will," the older son, Tenzin, answered quickly, sensing that his father held a special feeling for this task.

The little one caught his brother's excitement and rushed forward to hug Dorje's knees. "Me too, me too," Gyamo cried, not wanting to be left out.

Dorje and his two sons walked out the door and followed a path into the woods. Years before, Dorje had taken the path to the woods to bury the placentas of these sons. If they had had more land, they could have buried the placenta near the house, but it was important to find a place where it would not be contaminated by wild animals who might dig it up.

If the placenta became contaminated, it would be considered bad luck for the family and for the baby. The day before, Dorje had visited an astrologer who told him that today would be an auspicious day to take the placenta away.

When they had walked a good distance into the woods, through thick pine trees that gave off a fragrant pine scent in the hot sun, Dorje picked a place that felt appropriate and they started to dig. "As a sign of respect, I am burying the placenta deep in the ground," Dorje explained to his sons. Tenzin struggled with the big shovel, trying to dig his share of the hole. Though Dorje didn't mark the place in any way or need to remember where it was buried, he had a great respect for the placenta itself as a physical and symbolic connection between Lhamo and the new Dolma Tsering. Burying it in the ground bonded his child to the earth: the child's most valuable possession to date, the placenta that nurtured her for nine months, would now nurture the earth into which it was laid.

After the burial, father and sons walked back toward the house, and Dorje's thoughts moved away from the special task, which had been successfully completed. By the time he greeted Lhamo and an exuberant Dolma Tsering, he was caught up in the more immediate concerns of living. He did not even tell Lhamo where he buried the placenta, and soon neither of them thought about it again.

Naming the Baby

Traditionally, families seldom name the baby themselves. Instead, parents generally request a name from a high lama. This request represents their acceptance of the greater spiritual force of which both they and the baby are a part. Receiving a name from a lama further bonds a child with the realm of deities and the spiritual dimension of his or her Tibetan heritage. A name indicates that the child has a place in the Tibetan culture and a role to fulfill during this lifetime.

If possible, Tibetan parents prefer to have their babies named by His Holiness the Dalai Lama, the highest lama; otherwise, they will take their child to another lama to be named. Other parents may name the child themselves; sometimes they will name the child after the day on which it was born, or else they may choose a name at random. For instance, if the child is born on Saturday, *Pen-pa* in Tibetan, the parents may name the child Penpa Dhondup for a boy or Penpa Dolma for a girl. Many young people have the name Tenzin after the current Dalai Lama, Tenzin Gyatso. But generally people want a reincarnated lama to give the child a name in order to minimize the possibility of sickness or other unpleasant incidents befalling the child.

Even prebirth or womb names may be sought from incarnate lamas by anxious parents. When a family encounters difficulty in bringing up children—for instance, if more than one dies—then such strange names as *Khyi-kyag,* which literally means "dog shit," may be given to the survivor or the next child born. They believe that this will ward off future misfortunes for them because such an ugly name will repel harmful spirits who might otherwise be attracted to the child. When a lama determines that a child is safe, a new name may be given.

Unless the child becomes seriously ill or seems to have particularly bad luck, he or she will usually keep the name they are given. If inauspicious events occur, the parents may go again to the lama to receive a fresh name, representing a symbolic starting over. A mother might also take a sick baby to a lama or ask a lama to come to the house for a traditional healing and prayer. As mentioned, when a child is seriously ill, a lama may propose a change in its name. On rare occasions, when a child or an adult was thought almost dead, but came back to life, the name *Shi-log,* which literally means "return from death," is given.

Most Tibetans are given two names. They will commonly be called by both names, as Rinchen Lhamo is, or by one or the other of the two names—whichever their family uses naturally. Although Tibetan families have surnames to identify a particular family, traditionally only aristocratic families used their surnames. Since most Tibetan communities are small and cooperative, even those in exile in India, everyone knows everyone and who is related to whom. Trends have changed today, however, and many younger generation Tibetans have added and regularly use their surnames. Since Tibetans have made their way to the West, they have placed greater emphasis on carrying a last name so Westerners would know how to refer to them and they could become integrated into Western ways.

Lhamo: Mother and Daughter

A few days after Dolma Tsering's welcoming ceremony, the house was quiet and Lhamo, Dorje, Yeshe, Tenzin, and Gyamo had settled into a new routine with the new baby. Lhamo sat cross-legged on her bed in the multipurpose main room, holding her baby girl in layers and layers of warm blankets and shawls. Confident that her baby was going to stay a girl, Lhamo now settled into caring for the demands of her infant and carrying on the activities of the house from her position on the bed. There she could nurse Dolma Tsering whenever she was hungry, lay her daughter down to sleep right next to her, keep track of the other children, and drink tea with visiting friends. Continuing her daily activities with her baby beside her fostered a thorough and intimate bonding between the two of them.

Yeshe, Lhamo's mother-in-law, lived with Dorje and Lhamo, adding both richness and warmth to their household. And Lhamo especially appreciated her mother-in-law's presence now, with the new baby. Yeshe was adept at balancing her nurse's work at the clinic with her traditional grandmother's role as the nurturing caretaker for all the children, including newborn Dolma Tsering. As Yeshe poured their tea, Lhamo put a fresh dab of butter on the soft spot on the top of Dolma Tsering's head and then on her own head and temples. She would do this each day for seven to ten days after the birth. According to tradition, the butter would keep out the rlung, or winds. If the winds got in, it was believed they could cause serious trouble and illness later on in the child's life.

After finishing their hot buttered tea, Yeshe went to the clinic, and Lhamo prepared Dolma Tsering for her daily bath. Holding the baby upright in a blue plastic tub, Lhamo gently washed her daughter. Dolma Tsering loved the warm water, happily gurgling and enjoying these intimate moments with her mother. When Dolma Tsering was ready to get out of the water, Lhamo lay her on a warm blanket and gently patted her dry. She then placed Dolma Tsering in a pool of sunshine coming in through the window. "When it is warm, we will go outside," she promised the baby. According to tradition, she knew that daily exposure to the sun was important for good health.

In the patch of sunshine, Lhamo gave Dolma Tsering her daily massage, gently rubbing sesame oil all over her tiny body and exercising her legs and arms. Dolma Tsering smiled, her curious brown eyes watching Lhamo's every move. Not only did it feel good, but the massage helped to keep her circulation flowing and added flexibility to her developing muscles. The neighboring Indians also had a long tradition of massaging their babies. In the mornings and early evenings, Lhamo had often seen Indian mothers sitting in the sun with their newborns in their laps, massaging and exercising their small muscles. Even Lhamo's friends who had moved to Western countries made a point of giving their children sun baths and taking them out daily for long walks to get fresh air.

After her massage, Lhamo sat near Dolma Tsering for a few last minutes in the strong sun, allowing the baby's skin to absorb the oil and warmth. Lhamo looked forward to the time each day when she would bathe and sun Dolma Tsering. It was always a peaceful time in the routine of the day. Whereas the welcoming ceremony had been a special event to introduce Dolma Tsering to her community, the daily baths formed a solid foundation of bonding between mother and daughter upon which larger events of Dolma Tsering's life would rest.

A Sense of Touch

I had watched Lhamo and Palmo each give their newborns morning sun baths and massages many times, and each time I could practically feel the depth of the bond between mother and child that this simple act induced. Touch includes the touch of the mother and close family, massage with oil from plants and minerals, and the touch of the sun, with its warmth and light and energy. Often a Tibetan mother will put her child on her back and take the child almost everywhere, even when she is working in the fields or doing road work. Bodily touch is seen as crucial to a child's full development and proper bonding with its family.

The Dalai Lama emphasizes that bodily touch is crucial to the development of a child's brain. The Dalai Lama was born and bonded with his mother in much the same fashion as most babies. It wasn't until he was recognized as the reincarnation of the Thirteenth Dalai Lama that he began to bond more with his spiritual path and leadership duties than with his parents.

Remembering a time when he still lived with his family, the Dalai Lama spoke with me, with his distinctive candor, concerning the intricacies of human relationship. He focused on what makes the bond between a mother and infant so special. "The first act after birth," he said, "is the child sucking the mother's milk. If the mother's mood remains angry, I think the milk will not flow properly. The mother's life in this way is reflected in the child. The child's sight is developed and recognized, but there is still a desire, in the body itself, to have some kind of closeness. It is with physical touch that a child survives and the brain develops."

"In my own family," he continued, his eyes twinkling merrily, "my father had a very short temper and my mother was very kind. In the early part of life I learned more from my father. Then in the later part of life I learned more from my mother. I learned from both sides, very painfully."

After a good laugh at these amusing memories of his relationship with his own parents, the Dalai Lama continued, "Bonding is very important. Mentally, the method of bonding is not very clear, but physically, it is simple: babies receive bodily touching from their mothers. Physical touch is a very crucial factor for healthy development, including the development of brain cells in the first few weeks. In that moment of bodily touch, if something is negative, it is very harmful and damaging to the development of the brain. It has nothing to do with religion. It is simply that, as human beings, our physical condition requires touch to develop fully."

Tibetans naturally incorporate touch into their childraising practices, thus enhancing the physical, emotional, and spiritual growth of their children. Tibetan society facilitates both bodily touch and bonding as babies and children are easily welcomed into almost all activities and situations. Mothers and babies are rarely separated. A baby rides on a mother's back or in her arms almost everywhere she goes. It is easy for a mother to continue her normal pattern of movement and work with her baby on her back. If the baby cries or fusses, a mother can nurse it in just about any social situation without embarrassment.

For his part in bonding with Dolma Tsering, Dorje held his daughter or carried her about in a shawl on his back. Rocking her or walking, he sang her his favorite melodious mantras, such as the Green Tara mantra OM TARE TUTTARE TURE SOHA, for protection, as his father had sung to him. He was also the one to offer her a first taste of tsampa. Dorje, like many Tibetan fathers, was actively involved in the care and extra chores a new baby brings and was busy doing much of the washing, cleaning, cooking, rocking the baby, bringing tea to Lhamo and visitors, and running the household so that Lhamo could rest and devote most of her time to the newborn.

Other adults and older children in the Tibetan community are eager to lend a hand in childcare. And parents aren't made to feel bad if their child cries at an inopportune time. Many other family members and friends hold the baby when they can, serving to expand the infant's bodily contact and physical bonding with others in the community.

Pilgrimage and Initiation

In the Tibetan view, bonding between parents and child lasts for many lifetimes. As discussed in the chapter on preconception, before a child is even conceived, it is believed that there is a bond between a child and his or her particular parents. And this bond causes a magnetic attraction that draws the child into its mother's womb. Once a child has entered the womb, the bonding between the mother and baby is greatly enhanced and is nurtured throughout the pregnancy, through the birth process, during the time directly after birth, through infancy, and well beyond childhood.

I saw the strength of these bonds as I watched my friends Yeshe and Rinchen Lhamo, Choeling, and Gyatso in their grandmother, aunt, and uncle roles as well as their mother, sister, and brother relationships. Each of these stages, each relationship, has a particular feel and intensity that adds to the overall bonding process. I felt comforted by the thought that the bonds I viewed here would continue through the whole cycle, from birth through death and beyond.

This larger vision of bonding came home to me one day in Dharamsala as I watched the interaction of a grandmother and grandchild. I had stopped to admire a museum room at the library, where hundreds of statues of deities, tankas, and Tibetan religious ritual instruments are kept. While admiring them, I noticed an elderly woman with a baby in her arms walking around in a clockwise direction, looking at the statues, much as I was. At each statue, the elderly woman bowed her head in respect. Then she would lightly touch her head to the object or the glass case in which it was preserved.

The baby, too, was brought into this prayer. The grandmother lifted the baby toward each statue, gently touching her head to the glass case so the baby could also receive the blessing of each statue. The baby seemed to enjoy the process, eyes wide as she came close to the glass, blinking once or twice as she made contact. Even at this young age, the baby was brought up to pray in this way. The grandmother, in a gentle way, was introducing the baby to the deities that would protect her and her family as the infant grew into childhood and adulthood. The grandmother was also showing the baby how to pay proper respect to the deities by having the baby's head touch the glass, as well as her own.

Later, I thought about this moving scene and how many different ways there are to bind children to their family, community, and heritage. This grandmother and grandchild demonstrated how an infant's extended family, as well as the Tibetan Buddhist deities, are important and sustaining forces in a child's life. This child, like Dolma Tsering, is an individual with her own ideas and life ahead of her, but she is also an integral member of a large network of family and friends whose lives will affect her and who will in turn be affected by her life. Just as these people expect her to be responsible and caring toward them, they will be responsible and caring toward her. Even as tiny newborns, these children are part of a dynamic Tibetan community that has certain rules and privileges with which they are already intimately entwined.

Touch, sunlight, and cleansing are combined in an outdoor bath.

6:   Infancy

Gems of Tibetan Wisdom in Infancy

◊   *Babies retain special gifts, sensitivities, and capacities that adults no longer have; for instance, it is believed that children can see and hear things that adults cannot perceive.*

◊   *The physical and spiritual realms of life are naturally integrated, and the daily unfolding of life is sacred.*

◊   *Nursing mothers continue the prebirth prohibitions against using alcohol, nicotine, and caffeine, understanding that these substances, passed to their babies through their milk, could damage their children's bodies and minds.*

◊   *Each new learning, such as the first smile, the first step, the first word, is seen as unique. Because each fresh discovery about life invigorates an infant's energy and contains the motivation for its next step in maturation, it is vital to notice and recall these learnings.*

Sonyal: The Toddler and the Fly

Tashi watched his youngest daughter, Sonyal, with love and amusement as she hesitatingly and then with bursts of exuberance, crossed the living room toward the door. The toddler wore a Tibetan *chuba*, a miniature of her mother's dress. And in her tightly closed fist she clutched a fly. Just a few moments ago, Tashi had caught the fly and carefully placed it in his daughter's hand. With fond attention he had closed each of her tiny fingers around the visiting fly. Then, kneeling slowly, he instructed her to take it to the door to let it go, fostering in her a respect for all living creatures, one of the primary values of Tibetan Buddhism.

"There you go, take it outside," her father encouraged her gently. Then he sat back, cross-legged, on the thick wool rug that covered his bed. "But be careful. We don't want to harm it."

The child's chubby legs faltered, but she persevered in her mission to free the fly to the outdoors. Soon though, staring at her fist, she became increasingly inquisitive about how the fly was faring. She tried to peek inside her hand, which was clamped shut like a tenacious clam.

"No, no. Take it to the door," her father urged. "If you try to look at it, it will go away."

The girl looked back at her father and her dark eyes grew wide with indecision. She was only three feet from the open door. Her concern for the welfare of the fly, however, was too great. She slowly loosened her fingers, opened the tiny fist, and peered into the cage of her palm. Immediately, the fly shot out of her hand and flew to the far corner of the living room.

"Ah, now it's gone," Tashi laughed as he saw her surprise. The girl stared at her open, empty palm, looked up at her father, then stared back at her palm. She charged to the door and looked all around to see if the fly had somehow already made it to freedom. Not finding it there, she turned and ran to her father's lap. Hugging her, he laughed softly and kissed the top of her head.

In helping Sonyal free the fly, Tashi tried to teach her to feel a sense of caring and respect for all life, including even the life of a small fly. And as Sonyal grew older, Tashi would introduce her to his people's way of thinking through daily experience. For him, life was a continuation of other lives and part of an intricately woven web of relationships. Thus, creation of a life grew from one event to another. Through the sharing of life's stories as a series of interrelated lives, even the very young could come to understand the interdependence of all existence. A fly is a fly. It does what it does, and its life is respected. And so it can be with humans who are loved, protected, and gently guided to do the right thing.[42]

But in the meantime, it was enough that Sonyal insisted that they look once again for the fly in the corner. It was enough that she wanted to help a tiny fly in its escape to the morning sky.

The Six Stages of Infancy

Infancy is a dynamic time for both families and communities. Infants grow quickly, their bodies and their minds developing at a rapid pace. Bonding between parents and baby grows stronger and deeper as the baby establishes a place in the family and in the community. Accelerated learning continues as the infant begins to use mind, muscles, eyes, legs, arms, hands, head, face, and vocal chords to express thoughts and feelings and to move through the world. Many Tibetans believe that when babies are little, their future personality can be determined and the lines of character can be developed. The first few weeks after birth, I saw my friends in Dharamsala settle into routines with their new infants, babies and families alike becoming familiar with the changing patterns of care, sleeping and waking, nursing, and watching the new world.

One account of traditional Tibetan childcare identifies six stages in an infant's development. It is common and considered very important for Tibetan parents and other caregivers to recognize and facilitate these milestones. During the first stage, at around five months old, the child waves and reaches out to connect physically and emotionally with his or her parents. During the second stage, after about six months, a baby is able to sit up and gain a new perspective and interest in his or her surroundings. After about eight months, a child's teeth begin to come in, which heralds the beginning of the third stage. At this time, the child must learn to deal with pain inside the mouth—the mouth has, up to this point, been a primary locus of pleasure in interacting with the baby's mother and the world. During the fourth stage, after nine months, the infant begins to crawl and develops a new mobility apart from his or her mother. Standing and walking, which begins after a year, is the fifth stage, and this new activity gives the infant further independence and freedom of movement. The sixth and final stage of infancy, which occurs within two years, features the child's growing ability to enunciate and say simple words such as "A-ma" and "A-pa" (mother and father).

The folklorist Thubten Sangay has written about the significance of a child's first words in the Tibetan tradition. "According to an old belief, if the child's first word is 'A-ma' or 'Ma' it will be separated from its mother first. It will be separated from its father first if its first word is 'A-pa' or 'Pa.' The best word the child could utter first is 'A-ni' which means aunt."[43]

In the Tibetan tradition, there are other special landmarks in an infant's development, such as the first time the child sucks milk from the mother's breast, the occurrence of the child's first smile, and the emergence of the baby's first tooth. Along with the six main stages of growth, these physical signals of inner development and the child's growing capacity for interactions and relationships are considered to have a deeper spiritual significance.

Rituals During Infancy

As in all aspects of the Tibetan birth tradition, there are many rituals to ensure the physical and spiritual well-being of infants. Many of these traditions are steeped in ancient Tibetan practices, while others bear a marked resemblance to modern infant care practices. A number of these rituals and traditions are performed specifically for the health and safety of infants and the avoidance of *dip* or unhealthy influences. These traditions are most often passed down in families and community as folklore or colorful stories as a part of the oral tradition, or, less often, they may be found in Tibetan medical texts or written accounts of the Tibetan lifestyle.

Spiritual beliefs such as the Tibetan belief in reincarnation are often reflected in these traditions. For example, Tibetan folklore explains that infants who have a strong grip actually possess a wish-fulfilling gem (a mythological gem that can grant any wish) in their hands and do not want anyone to take it away. This belief demonstrates an accepted understanding among community members that babies come from somewhere else, have had previous lives, and will protect the "gems" they have been gifted with at birth and preserve them for their new families. Even though the newborn is small and helpless at birth, the gem represents the continuity the baby maintains with previous lives and the talents, wisdom, and experiences from other lives that will influence this life.

For many new parents and their friends, watching the types of faces infants frequently make is a continual source of entertainment. Babies have the most wonderful expressions, especially when their faces become contorted in intense concentration and feeling. The medical reason for these contorted faces is wind in the intestines, caused by awkward sucking or feeding that causes pain and frowning. The Tibetan folklore explanation for this phenomenon is much more colorful. The story is that this discomfort is caused by a dwarfish creature called *Thep-rang*, a small mischievous fairy-tale being who sometimes irritates babies and makes them frown and look unhappy. And then when Thep-rang plays with the babies, they smile. Another explanation is that babies look unhappy when they remember their terrible experiences in the hell realms during bardo. And when they remember happier times, they smile.

In another example of traditional Tibetan folklore, it is said that an infant is looked after by an invisible pig and an invisible monkey who take turns tending to the infant on alternate days. On the pig's day, it is believed that the child's flesh grows and that the child is quieter and sleeps better. On the monkey's day, when the bones are forming and developing, the baby experiences pain and consequently does not sleep well and cries more often. Assigning the growth of the flesh and the bones to a pig and a monkey suggests that infant development is not a responsibility that is limited to family members; human and nonhuman beings are intermingled in the cosmology of the child's life. Later in childhood, when adults include the presence of these beings in their stories, a child understands that his or her life includes more than human experience and interactions.

Another bit of folklore recommends that a baby who is teething should be kept from seeing pregnant women. Otherwise, the child's teeth will not grow properly until the pregnant woman has delivered her baby. This is an ancient Tibetan custom from the shamanistic, pre-Buddhist *Bön* tradition. It is said that when a young peacock first develops its crown feathers and when a baby first develops teeth, they both experience pain throughout their bodies. It is recommended that medicine boiled with honey and left to cool can be applied over the whole body in order to quicken the growth of the teeth. Remedies are offered for any illness arising from teething.

While boys and girls are treated similarly and are protected by the same rituals at this early age, Thubten Sangay describes in the following passage one of the traditional practices during infancy that marks the difference between a boy and a girl:

> It is customary to have the baby's ears pierced at eight months. A boy has his right ear pierced and a girl her left. According to the childcare scriptures, a little vermilion (red powder) should be rubbed into the lobe. The ear is then pierced from the back at the thinnest point, using a needle threaded with dog hair. The hole should be treated with a little oil. Piercing the ear is a ceremony performed mainly for auspiciousness, but if the child is a recognized incarnation or if it is destined to be ordained, it is not done. [44]

Although the ear-piercing is a quick process, details and rituals are given careful attention. The practice is not as common as it used to be, perhaps because of the influence of contact with Westerners and Indians.

After the first birthday of a child, it is a common custom for all of his or her hair to be cut off. This hair is called the "birth-hair" and is considered rather unclean and an impediment to the natural growth of the child's hair. This cutting of the birth-hair is believed to ensure good hair growth later on. Interestingly, this belief regarding cutting hair is in contrast to that of other cultures, like the Sikhs in India, who place such value on their hair that they never cut it throughout their entire lives. And in the United States, baby hair is often considered special, and a parent may feel sad when they cut their child's hair for the first time as it symbolizes the child is no longer a baby.

Thubten Sangay tells of another folk ritual that parents may perform to encourage perambulation if a child is not walking after a year. First, the parents seat the child backwards on a white cow or a yak. While holding the child up, the nurse urges the animal to move forward, shouting an enthusiastic "da-ya, da-ya." This is considered encouragement for the child to walk independently. Not only does this describe an innovative way to bring about walking, it also indicates that some children were raised by nurses. Books about traditional Tibet often refer to children's nurses, but I never witnessed this arrangement in Tibetan refugee communities. Perhaps this tradition is prevalent in texts because the few Tibetans who have written about their early lives in Tibet tend to be from the upper class. Now, however, few Tibetans, whether in Tibet or exile, have the financial resources for nurses, though many have the help of grandparents and other extended family members in raising their children.

In *Daughter of Tibet*, Rinchen Dolma Taring describes other traditional infant care and rituals that have been interrupted since the Chinese invasion in 1959. For instance, in the second week after birth, parents traditionally took their baby to Jokhang (the biggest temple in Lhasa) for the child to pay his or her first homage to Lord Buddha. The child, wrapped in a soft maroon blanket with a big silk patch in the center, especially made by the mother-in-law, was carried on the nanny's back.[45] A little black mark was put on the child's nose for protection from evil spirits during this visit or any other outdoor activities. Gold and silver charm boxes, a tortoise shell, and a picture of the Wheel of the Universe were sewn on a brocade belt and put around the child to protect the little life from all harm.

A lingering folk belief is that it is safer to keep babies at home at night. Parents rarely take their children out at night unless they must. And if they must, soot from the hearth is commonly put on the baby's nose and chest and drawn upward in a dark line, using the third finger. Even during the day, babies who are away from home may be seen wearing a smudge of soot on their nose for extra protection from the spirits that may be lurking in wait for them. It is believed that a soot or charcoal smudge serves to detract from a baby's beauty so that bad spirits won't think the baby is too pretty and thus cause harm to the child.

This safeguarding custom has its roots in an ancient legend about a mother who had to leave her house late at night with her baby. It was well known that evil spirits were particularly dangerous to babies at night. And, sure enough, a little while after she left the house an evil spirit began chasing her. She ran and ran and soon came to a bridge. As she ran across the bridge she was able to scoop a little charcoal in her hands and put a dot of it on her baby's nose. She then hid at the far end of the bridge as she knew she couldn't outrun the spirit any longer. The spirit came quickly over the bridge and ran right past her, not seeing the baby because it was hidden by the charcoal smudge. From that time on, parents have put black soot smudges on their babies' noses to protect them if they have to take them out at night and sometimes even during the day.

I spoke to a Tibetan woman in Dharamsala who knew firsthand about the serious belief regarding soot dots. One day, she had visited a friend, lost track of time, and arrived at home when it was late and very dark. She had forgotten all about the traditional rituals to keep her baby safe at night. "When I arrived home," she said, "my brother-in-law was very upset that I had jeopardized the baby's safety by not taking the precaution of putting the soot smudge on her nose as soon as night fell." She explained that, like many Tibetans her age in India, she sometimes forgets about these customs. "It's not that I don't believe in them. It's just that they are not as important to me as they are to my brother-in-law, who came more recently from Tibet, and other people from the older generations."

Many of the Tibetans in Dharamsala between twenty and forty years old echoed this attitude, saying that they neither believed nor disbelieved the traditional superstitions. They know these beliefs and practices are part of their culture—their older relatives have usually talked about them a great deal and stressed their importance—so they comply with them when they can. Even when children are brought up as refugees, the culture is passed on to them. Elders speak of the traditions and children listen, hearing bits and pieces of this and that ritual, and soon the children know the customs. And soon after that, they begin to believe in them. Although, busy with other things to do, the younger generations often don't take time to do the rituals properly. Unless, that is, something goes wrong or a child becomes sick. Then many Tibetans who don't usually follow these rituals will make the time to do them.

Palmo told me a story that echoed this tendency. "One time, my neighbor's baby developed an eye infection. The baby was two-and-a-half weeks old and the parents should have had blessed water on hand long before—but they never got around to it and didn't really believe in it anyway. But when the baby was sick, they got that water fast!" She laughed. "The husband went right out to get a big pot of blessed water from a rinpoche to make the eye clean. Young people still learn about these beliefs. They hear bits and pieces from their parents and others, and that knowledge and belief slowly sinks in. But it takes a bit more than belief sometimes to make the rituals a regular part of life."

The older Tibetans who have made the long journey to Dharamsala from Tibet have indeed provided a rich knowledge of the traditional beliefs. Yeshe described to me several favorite customs of traditional infant care that she grew up with. For instance, in one tradition, parents avoid putting socks and shoes on a baby before it is one year old. In her part of Tibet, they also avoided dressing a baby with a hat or cap before it is five years old. To do either of these things is considered inauspicious.[46] Of course the baby is kept warm by thorough blanketing. In another belief, when a father or mother returns from a distant place, they should not go straight to greet their infant children. If the child is picked up immediately after they arrive, it is believed that the unclean air the parent has brought from afar can cause *dip*, the invisible pollution, which would bring on sickness or transmit a curse to the child. Instead, they should rest so as to cool down the body and then take a bath and wash up. These types of rituals and beliefs have largely died out in modern Tibetan culture. But even if they are no longer practiced, the essence of these customs and traditions are familiar to most Tibetans.

Early Teaching

As the bonding between mother and child grows from birth, it continues to develop during infancy. All family members help to take care of and raise the child, but an infant usually grows primarily in relationship with the mother, especially at the beginning of life. Mother and child come closer emotionally through every activity: feeding, massage, sunning, holding, and the mother's constant physical closeness to the baby. The mother cuddles and strokes the child, calls the baby by name, makes tender sounds, and imitates the child. A baby, beginning to recognize his or her mother, will begin to stretch his or her arms out in welcome when the mother approaches.

Normally at about eight months, the child can sit up. Soon after, when the baby starts crawling, the mother will create a space and sit nearby. The baby begins to crawl away, look back at her, and then crawl back. The mother welcomes the child back, holding out her arms, ready with a hug and a pat. At about a year, the mother helps the child learn to walk. As in many Western traditions, the whole family becomes very excited when the child takes his or her first step.

In teaching a child to talk, many Tibetan parents begin by identifying members of the family. Relatives are pointed out to the baby—not at first by name, but by relationship. In this early teaching, a parent takes the child to the shrine in the family shrine room, points to the statues and tankas of deities, and teaches the child to give respect by holding his or her hands together and bowing the head forward. Of course, the child watches the family in many other customs and follows what they do.

Toilet training often begins with associations by sound. The mother makes a specific sound and then the child slowly identifies that sound with the need to use the toilet pot. Soon the child learns to make these sounds, and in response the mother points to a place for the child to go, or brings the pot herself. By one-and-a-half or two years old, the child does this independently.

Dr. Rapgay's mother, Pasang Lhamo, was a midwife, first in Tibet and later on in Dharamsala. In her early seventies, she moved to California to enjoy the company of her sons and grandchildren. I asked her about her experiences raising and teaching very young children. I asked her what she would most want her grandchildren who are in the United States to carry forward from the Tibetan ways.

She considered my question thoughtfully. "I teach them some Tibetan," she answered. "And when the lamas or His Holiness come to California, I dress the children in Tibetan clothing and take them to see these holy men. And I often take the children to visit my shrine room so that they can begin to identify the deities. The littlest one already joins his hands and bows," she added proudly. I had seen toddlers throughout the Tibetan communities in India and in Tibetan households in the United States make this same gesture. It is one of the first acknowledgments of their culture that Tibetans learn—wherever they are.

Infant Disease, Maternal Postpartum Depression, and Treatments

According to some Tibetan traditions, the main causes of infant disease and disorders are the mother's dietary regularities and irregularities, behavioral practices, and psychological factors. And if the mother has been suffering from any diseases, the baby is likely to be affected as well.

Tibetan tradition recognizes the existence in a new mother of postpartum depression and defines it as a "deficiency of life-sustaining wind." Life-sustaining wind is the energetic flow that is primarily responsible for all natural processes in humans. When the energy becomes deficient, below its normal level, depression is one of the likely disorders at a psychological level. Physically, the person loses energy, becomes easily fatigued, and dislikes movement, activity, or too much stimulation. Emotionally, there is loss of confidence and a loss of faith, first in oneself and then in others. Denial or the concealing of such feelings may lead to a sense of guilt, a state of inattentiveness, dullness, insensitivity, and even a loss of sensation.

Treatment for such a condition in Tibetan medicine includes pulse examination and questioning, body massage with special herbal oils, acupressure, and herbal steaming to promote relaxation and remove toxins. Healing visualizations, breathing meditation, chanting of the mantra OM AH HUM, and nutritional and herbal supplements are also recommended. Although a mantra works at several levels, it can be said that OM purifies all the negative actions committed through the body, AH through speech, and HUM through the mind, or attitude and thoughts. In the Tibetan view there is no separation between body and mind and therefore no separation between medicine and psychology. Postpartum depression is taken seriously, and it is considered important to treat the mother's condition for the sake of her own health as well as the effect her depression may have on her infant and the rest of the family.

In the Tibetan medical tradition, there is a common infant illness called "falling down of the liver." Its symptoms are similar to pneumonia, and sometimes older people get it as well. It is extremely difficult to cure and causes tremendous pain to a child. Common symptoms are diarrhea that is a greenish color, fever, and blackening of the forehead.

Traditionally, it is believed that the illness is caused by curses or a sudden fright. Besides short rituals and prayers, treatment involves regrouping the fallen or spread-out liver with the help of a religious object, the *me-long*, or mirror, which is a round disk made of bronze.

Dorje had observed cases of this illness at Delek Hospital. "I have seen children with this illness forced to receive painful injections and breathe hot steam. And all were treated in this manner without success. Only then did they allow the child to be treated by the traditional method. The child invariably was cured and went home as cheerful as ever." After this illness, as a precaution, the mother is advised not to jerk or move the child violently as that can cause a relapse of the illness. And, to be safe, the child is treated at least twice a day for two days.

Diarrhea, another common infant ailment, may be treated with mantra. Three long protection cords are entwined to form one cord. This is cut in two, and twenty knots are tied in each. The mantra YAMA CHO is recited a hundred times for each cord and blown on them. One cord is tied around the baby's neck and the other around its wrist. With vomiting, the same ritual is performed using the mantra YAMA SHIK. Diarrhea associated with heat, inflammation, or fever is red, brown, yellow, or green. Diarrhea associated with cold or chills is usually white. The classification of hot and cold diseases is at the root of Tibetan medical treatment, and is determined by complex and discerning methods. [47]

In the Tibetan tradition, it is believed that vomiting is usually caused by cold bile. Accompanying symptoms are the inability to digest mother's milk or food, yellowish eyes, and a distended stomach. This is treated by wafting the smoke of a burning mixture of medicinal substances over the baby's stomach or by giving the child medicine mixed in fresh meat juice. If the baby vomits green mucus or mother's milk, medicine is given in rice porridge. If the baby vomits the porridge, a small fast is recommended. If none of these treatments are successful, a *moxa* on the crown of the head is used to cure the sickness. Moxa is a medicinal stick made of compressed herbs which is lit and held about an inch over the skin to give healing heat and purifying smoke.

According to Tibetan medical scripture, a baby with diarrhea should not be given meat or barley porridge, but should be fed instead on Indian or Tibetan wheat or rice flour porridge that is well cooked with fresh butter, sweet powdered cheese, and a little salt and then left to cool until it thickens slightly. If already weaned, the baby should be given cracked wheat porridge with cheese and salt two or three times a day. It is believed that these porridges will cure the diarrhea very easily. Rice porridge is used to treat diarrhea associated with heat and wheat porridge is used for diarrhea associated with cold.

Infants suffer from many kinds of pustule diseases, including measles. Some of these are contracted only once, while others recur. Measles and smallpox are among the childhood illnesses that do not recur. In Tibetan and Western medicine, a great deal of interest has been shown in the treatment of smallpox. Many cures now exist and the use of vaccine is also widespread. Measles, however, are still widespread among young children. While it appears that their treatment is not mentioned in the traditional medical tantras, the Blue Sapphire oral tradition scripture mentions that their symptoms are similar to a feverish chill and that as long as precautions are taken there is no need for special treatment.

It is recommended that sour foods like alcohol, sour cheese, garlic, onions, red pepper, and salt are to be avoided because it is believed that they cause heat in the body or worsen the illness. Salt in particular should be avoided as it is believed that it may cause pimples to grow inside the eyelids. The oral tradition scriptures mention seven kinds of measles, yet these may be condensed into two varieties, red and white. The symptoms in general are similar to any contagious disease but specifically manifest as small pimples that appear over the whole body when the illness breaks out. The armpits and groin also become hot. After a day or so, most of the pimples dry up. But until this occurs the child should be kept warm. In certain parts of Tibet, a traditional method is used to bring out the pimples quickly. First, the foods listed above are avoided, then thick barley beer is rubbed into the child's body for two days during which he or she is kept very warm. This brings out the pimples, and once that occurs the child is given nourishing food. [48]

The Tibetan medical system places great emphasis on the preparation of medicines. There are traditional techniques to prepare preventive medicines for infants. In one remedy, a black, soot-like substance and yellow moss—both found on a black rock facing north, untouched by the rays of the sun—are burnt together with two or three strands of hair from the crown of the mother's head to form an ash which is then given to the child with a little barley. It is believed that this will guard the child from illness for a year. It is also believed that a mixture of musk, sweet-bear flag (Acorus calamus), and molasses given to the child with barley beer ensures not only vajra-like health but freedom from illness and harm by spirits for twelve years. These preparations are taken from *A Compendium of Precious Oral Teachings on the Science of Healing* by the doctor Do-karma Chö-gyal.[49]

Several Tibetan scholars—notably Thubten Sangay and Norbu Chophel Kharitsang—have recorded what they know of traditional Tibetan childcare practices. In a section entitled "Health of the Child," Thubten Sangay states the following:

> In the childcare scriptures it says: "For intelligence and long life, grind together medicines to form a fine mixture. Mix this with either honey or butter. If a little of this mixture is given each morning, intelligence and health will follow." The grinding needs to be done by someone skilled in the preparation of medicine; a doctor should be requested to do this. Certain substances wrapped to form a small bundle and tied around the baby's neck will guard it from the harms of earth gods, *nagas*, and spirits.[50]

Before the advent of vaccinations and other modern cures, disease and hardship took their toll on Tibetan children, indeed on the Tibetan population in general. Some children didn't survive the rigorous lifestyle and economics and the harshness of the terrain in Tibet. The average life span in Tibet in 1990 was fifty-four years. On the average, many families will have three to five children, and larger families will have twelve to fourteen. In the past, over half the babies died.

Palmo's family reflected the reality of these statistics. "In our family, my mother gave birth to fifteen children," she remembered. "Many babies died in childbirth or shortly after they were born. Because of unsanitary conditions, it is easy to catch infection. Few women die in childbirth, though. Of the many families I know, I don't know anyone who has." I had heard from a number of other sources that few women actually died in childbirth. It seems that while infection was a common cause of death for babies and young children, mothers were usually healthy through childbirth.

Spiritual Life and Reincarnation

In the Tibetan tradition, it is believed that babies may have special attributes or abilities that adults no longer possess, or that infants may have relations with supernatural elements. Often these are considered evil spirits. In some cases, a child is believed to be the reincarnation of a holy person, such as a lama or rinpoche. But ordinary children are ascribed these powers and abilities as well. All children are considered to be in a state of purity, and because of this purity they are able to see things that are part of other realms. A baby is so small, so new, that it is literally being reborn, starting afresh. According to this tradition, human beings retain this purity in infancy and early childhood—and then we spend the rest of our lives trying to get back to that purity and clarity.

It is believed that children remember their previous lives until they begin to stand, and that every time the child gets up and falls down, more past incarnations are forgotten and more is learned about this lifetime. When babies smile or cry in their sleep, it is said that is due to their connection to previous lives. Some babies begin to remember certain aspects from their previous lives as they get older. And it is in this remembering that the community is able to discover reincarnations of especially holy people. There are some children who seem to go on knowing these spiritual realms as they grow up. In some cases, they may have especially vivid dreams that seem to foretell the future. Even lamas, seeking visions for important decisions, may ask these children about their dreams. But most babies lose this ability as they get older; the mind becomes cloudy, and the purity vanishes.

An illustration of the way that young children are thought to have memories from previous lives is found in a story that is told about the present Dalai Lama. Even as a young child, he loved to pack things in a bag, as if to go off on a long journey, saying "I'm going to Lhasa!" He also insisted that he always be allowed to sit at the head of the table. Never did he show any fear of strangers. When he was not quite three years old, a member of the search party sent to find the reincarnation of the Thirteenth Dalai Lama visited his home. The young child recognized him and called out "Sera Lama, Sera Lama," naming the visiting lama's monastery. Then followed a number of tests of recognition, in which the child correctly identified from groups of similar items those that had belonged to his previous incarnation, saying "It's mine!"

Such statements and behaviors are seen by Tibetans as indications that the Dalai Lama could remember his previous life during the early years of his childhood. In the same way, many Tibetan children, not only incarnate lamas, are thought to be able to remember their previous lives, even though these memories fade as the children grow older.

Young faces of a new generation of Tibetans in exile.

7:   Early Childhood

Gems of Tibetan Wisdom through Early Childhood

◊   *Ritual celebration of significant steps in a child's development is a core value; it is essential to recognize each step, mark the quality of deep feeling, and honor a sense of connection to the sacred.*

◊   *A child has a natural phase of simplicity of mind before it is developmentally ready to interrelate experiences, senses, emotions, and thoughts with its situation and past experience. Some feel that this beginning mind allows the child to have communication with spirits that adults do not usually have.*

◊   *Tibetans emphasize teaching children through imitation, memorization, touch, and movement so the full meaning of the material can seep into consciousness intuitively as well as intellectually. Before the age of eight, the emphasis is on teaching the child to remember what he or she already knows from previous lives.*

◊   *The environment for learning needs to be clean, nurturing, and full of touch and a sense of the sacred. Mistakes should be corrected without judgment.*

◊   *Children are vulnerable to impressions and need to be protected and healed when they experience fearful or intruding images.*

◊   *Twenty-four childhood disturbances, including nightmares, images, and projections, are identified and effectively treated by lamas.*

◊   *Any health problem or injury may have at its root a combination of physical, emotional, mental, and spiritual causes; the Tibetan system of medicine analyzes the problem within the total system and is inclusive in its treatments.*

◊ *Compassion, honesty, and sharing are valued qualities in children and can be instilled in young children through their natural imitation of adults, through discipline as needed, and through recognition and celebration of prized behaviors.*

◊ *Harmony in relationships is highly valued; it is important to teach even very young children how to interact harmoniously, rather than competitively, with other children, adults, animals, insects, and all sentient life.*

◊ *From an early age, a child is taught about rebirth and the cyclic nature of life.*

◊ *To be part of a family, to have been given life by one's parents, is highly prized; to be part of a community of people who share life together at many levels is also considered sacred.*

Chime

Disheveled and crying, Chime limped into the local clinic, held up by two other seven-year-old girls. While running with a kite with her friends, she had painfully sprained her ankle, so the children had helped her to the clinic. As the girls came in, Dorje, the doctor on staff at the clinic, was talking about a medical case with Yeshe, his mother, who helped out at the clinic. But Dorje quickly turned his full attention to assessing the sprain, calming the children, and laying out preparations to bandage the injury. Yeshe recognized the girl as Tashi and Tsering's daughter and let Dorje know.

Dorje held the ankle, touching points on the surface of Chime's skin and joints and rotating her ankle while he checked its movement. Then he smiled reassuringly at Chime and asked her to tell him where it hurt. He checked her pulses, then told Yeshe which blessed pills to bring. He gave one to Chime, reminding her to keep it under her tongue.

Chime was shy at first, but became more inquisitive as she and her friends watched Dorje bind the ankle. "How long will I need the bandage?" she asked.

"It may be a while," Dorje said, "but come back in a week, and we'll know more then. You'll need to take good care of it so the muscles can grow strong again. And remember to take the blessed pills each day. Here is a little bag for them."

By this time, Chime looked none the worse for the accident and seemed ready to go back to playing with her friends. But Dorje warned her, after administering the bandage, that she would need to rest and not run so that the ankle would have a chance to heal.

"I'll walk with her back to her parent's house," Yeshe told Dorje. "I want to visit Tsering's new baby, and I'm sure Chime can use a little assistance climbing that steep hill with her sprained ankle."

"Very good. Now she'll have someone to make sure she doesn't go running off and forget to be careful," Dorje said, patting Chime affectionately on the head. "She is such a brave girl, and I am afraid she'll forget to be careful and just want to run home and tell everyone the story of her accident."

Chime beamed at him as she and Yeshe waved good-bye to Dorje and Chime's friends and set off up the hill. Talking excitedly, Chime explained her accident. "The sky and the kite were so beautiful, I stumbled over a rock I didn't see. I was scared to fall because then I'd lose the beautiful kite my father made for me. But my friends are taking care of it." As they walked, Chime eventually slowed down and asked to rest a few times. The excitement of visiting the clinic had worn off a little.

At one of the rest stops, they heard children's voices coming from behind them. Chime explained that many of her friends went to the Montessori school. Chime and Yeshe could hear the children chanting their lessons in a deep, flowing rhythm, echoing their teacher's words and sentences over and over again. "My brother has pages and pages of the ancient texts memorized," Chime said proudly. "He started when he was very young and every day he memorizes a little more. Now he really knows a lot. Have you ever been to the Tibetan Children's Village?" Chime plunged ahead to her next thought as they started up the hill again toward her house. "One of my best friends, Tsogyal, lives there. Even though she is an orphan, she has a wonderful family who takes care of her. She loves living there so much she told me she never wants to go anywhere else, even after she graduates."

"Yes, I've been there," Yeshe answered. "It's a beautiful village, tucked up on the mountainside. I've met some of the girls who went there and have now graduated and gone on to jobs and schools somewhere else. Like your friend, they thought they never wanted to leave because they had such a good time there." Yeshe smiled, thinking about the Children's Village. When the Tibetan community had first arrived in Dharamsala, the refugee orphans hadn't had an easy life. Now the Village was a model and inspiration for other refugee communities around the world. Yeshe felt comforted by the warmth of Chime's small hand, and the two smiled in unison as Chime pointed to a young lamb wobbling along beside its mother. Chime began to hum a tune that kept pace with their steps. Soon Yeshe joined in.

They had almost reached Chime's home, when Chime suddenly broke away with renewed energy and ran the last few yards, calling loudly for her mother, Tsering, to listen to her adventures of the day. Hearing the commotion, the other children came running to hear her story as well. Yeshe approached the door more sedately, a bit winded from her climb and looking forward to a cup of Tibetan hot butter tea.

Special care from the family and community, as well as from healing practitioners, can be counted on for small or more serious health problems. The same is true for other significant events in a child's life.

Celebration of Significant Events

In the Tibetan tradition, it is considered very important to mark significant events and important beginnings in all stages of early childhood. It is said that there is nothing in one's childhood that is more wonderful and unique than each new learning experience. Tibetans believe that the vitality of such memories from infancy allows an adult to reconnect with the purity of life and the experience of other realms, which in infancy are not yet forgotten. So recognizing special events in a child's life—such as the first smile, or the first time a baby claps his or her hands or stands up—and making the time and the effort to mark these events are believed to be instrumental in the physical, emotional, mental, and spiritual development of a child.

Tibetans do this naturally in their own gentle way. When a child does something for the first time, the family acknowledges the event, recognizing its uniqueness and valuing the feeling that accompanies it. Unobtrusively, they create a special quality in the situation so that the child can sense that something different is happening. If a parent, other adult, or older sibling is around, it is considered important that they notice the event, express their joy, and celebrate the event with an appropriate ritual. These are moments that can never be repeated. Children and parents can never return to the moment when a child smiles or walks for the first time. Tibetans believe that rituals help to enhance these special times and events and that special recognition gives these events a sense of sacredness. These rituals mark a milestone in a child's growth and demonstrate that a particular developmental landmark has been acknowledged.

Such rituals celebrate not only a single accomplishment but also a child's deepening hold on his or her new life. For instance, when Tibetans stamp or trace the syllable DHIH with a special herb or butter on the baby's tongue directly after birth, they are marking the cherished values in the consciousness of the newborn and its family. When a baby is fed solid food for the first time, there might also be an initiation of some sort, such as a recitation, because this symbolizes that the baby is moving into a new phase. Massage and bodily touch, which were discussed in the chapter on bonding, are also important initiations and can be easily introduced through a process of initiation or ritual. The first time a child receives a massage, parents may recite mantras, say a special prayer, or have the older brothers and sisters come out to participate. Tibetan mothers commonly create a ritual when the child takes its first step. While Western parents might not enact a ritual, they are usually alert to notice the event and the whole family becomes excited. Some parents will record these first steps in a book or journal and tell friends and other family members. This too is a way of recognizing the importance of a childhood event.

Stages of Growth in Early Childhood

Tibetans identify three main stages of development: from birth to eight years old, from eight to fourteen years, and from fourteen on. In Western psychology, the ages from one to five years old form the developmental phase of early childhood. In Tibetan psychology these years are also seen as very important. In this first stage, the child still retains a sense of purity and innocence. Gyatso once told me, "As adults, when we look at a book, the moment we see its color, its size, its title, we have already formed several preliminary opinions of it that will influence our intellectual opinions of it. But children don't do that; their minds are not clouded with previous associations to that object. There is natural innocence in taking it for what it appears to be. We believe children have this innocence until they are eight." After the age of eight, thinking becomes much more complex. The child is more intellectually able to recall learnings, relate them to current experience, and then make judgments. But a child needs to better understand the nature of relationships before these comparisons can begin. The whole complex character of experience develops in a child when he or she interrelates sense perceptions and emotions and thoughts with objects and situations.

If a child is discovered to be a reincarnation of a lama, it is considered important to start teaching him or her before the age of eight because this validates the discovery of the child in natural purity. According to the basic system for teaching young monks or nuns, a child who wants to be a monk or nun is provided the environment of the monastery or nunnery but not the discipline or academic rigor until the age of eight. The child's main area of emphasis is to memorize literature, but he or she is not expected to understand the content of the material. Until the student can analyze the texts, he or she will simply imitate teachers and enjoy the recognition, the repetition, and the rhythm. More intensive training develops after the child is eleven or twelve.

Childhood Spirit Disturbances

Along with purity and innocence, until the child is eight years old it is believed that the child's mind has a special clarity. Tibetans say that until the age of eight, a child's consciousness is so fluid and clear that things can come easily into it. As the child has not been "educated," there are not a lot of preconceptions and the mind has lots of room for projections. The Tibetans believe that this can result in what is called "spirit disorders." There is a whole section in Tibetan texts on archetypal kinds of images that sometimes emerge and seem to possess a child. The child sees, experiences, or hears these images and they may dominate the child's mind. (These images might be described as "invisible friends" or "monsters" in the West.) While the images are clear, the child might find it difficult to convey these images to most adults, as it is difficult for a child to make sense of what is happening.

The book *Illustrated Principles and Practices of Tibetan Medicine* uses text and illustrations to give an explanation of the types of spirit disorders that may possess a child. There are twenty-four spirit disorders listed in all, along with drawings of the types of images that are believed to possess children. Some images are shaped like animals. They may resemble a sheep's or bull's head; a rabbit, fox, horse, or dog; or owls, swans, or other birds.[51] All the animals belong to the same group, but they have different functions. The text also includes pictures of a female spirit, something like a vajra, and an indestructible cannon ball.

Spirits are categorized into two types: aggressive and nonaggressive. The less aggressive tend to be more "cold" in nature and the more aggressive are "hot" in nature. Some spirits are female, others are male. One, which is called a "hungry ghost," has a huge stomach and a very thin neck. The stomach offers a paradox: the "hungry ghost" wants to eat a lot but it doesn't have a throat or neck through which food can go, so it becomes very frustrated. Another type appears as a king. The king is a positive deity in the Tibetan mythology.

After the child sees these images for awhile, the Tibetans believe that the child begins to think he or she is that image. The child might acquire behavioral characteristics like those he sees in the spirits. This influence may be reflected in the child's actions, speech, and general behavior. The child will express him or herself more and more like these images. Some of the spirits may have a frightening and disturbing influence. A child might begin to acquire more violent or abnormal behavior, such as uncontrollable crying or tantrums. Oftentimes, these images begin to appear to a child during the night, in a nightmare or upon waking. A child may seem physically fine but suddenly wake up in the night with uncontrolled crying. Sometimes the child talks to the spirits. It could seem like a monologue, a mental dialogue, or as if the child were carrying on a conversation with someone.

It is not considered unusual to see this behavior in children. Nor is it necessarily considered bad. But, while a child may seem very attached to the spirit, it is not considered a healthy relationship. Though some of the images may sound as if they are positive, like the god images, at this age their appearance is generally disruptive. Before the age of eight, it is believed that a child's consciousness of self is not yet firmly in place and can be easily displaced if led off course. Tibetans feel that a child must be protected from this kind of illness.

Thubten Sangay writes on this subject in his article entitled "Tibetan Traditions of Childbirth and Childcare," from the journal *Tibetan Medicine*:

There are fifteen kinds of spirits that harm children: seven are male and eight are female. One is the ghost of an assassinated king who was reborn as a spirit because of his anger. Another is the ghost of a wicked woman, and yet another is a king of the *nagas*, or snakes. Signs that indicate harm from these spirits include sudden fear, much crying, especially in the early hours of the morning and evening, trembling, groaning, a disturbed sleep, lip-biting, scratching the mother or digging its nails into her, refusing to nurse, white eyes, frothing at the mouth, and fever. If these signs occur, a doctor should be consulted.

Strong food such as alcohol, meat, blood, and green vegetables should not be given. Feed the child instead, the three white foods: milk, curd, and butter. Special rituals may be performed, including the Three Part Ritual of the Water Offering, the Reading of the Five Great Mantras, and the ritual of the Hundred Meats and Hundred Foods in which effigies are made and given to the spirit. A wheel of protection may be tied to the child and, if possible, the ritual of *Do*, or *mdos*, [a cross formed of two small sticks, the ends of which are connected by colored strings, and used in various magical ceremonies] should be performed. If these are of no help, then according to the childcare scriptures, a powerful tantric master should be approached and requested to perform, among others, the Turning of the Wheel of

Fire together with the wrathful mantra and the ritual for Destroying the Demon Bird. Finally, a spiritual master with powers over mantra should be consulted again and again for advice. [52]

To protect the child from being frightened by the images, some Tibetan families put a black spot on the child's nose before he or she goes to bed. Traditionally, a parent would use his or her ring finger to put a line of black soot down the child's nose. It is believed that when an image sees something foreign in the hallway or on the child's body, like a smudge, the image is scared away by the strange black color on the nose and distance is created between the image and the child's psyche. This is another use of a black charcoal dot on a child's nose as a form of protection—just as it is used in infancy when the child goes out at night. It is interesting to note how many cultures have techniques to help a child sleep free from nightmares. In the United States, a blanket or favorite stuffed animal will often be used to help the child sleep soundly. The small bedtime ritual of putting the "protector" in place—whether it be a black dot or a stuffed animal—is usually enough security to calm a child's active mind. Of course there are many components, but the black spot is a common and seemingly effective ritual and has been passed down through many generations of Tibetan families. While it is commonly used for younger children, it is generally believed that a child no longer needs it after the age of six.

Tibetans believe that this trouble with spirits can be rectified by eliminating the image through ritual. If a ghost seems to be visiting a child, the parents may begin treatment by placing a black spot on the child's nose. But if the symptoms increase, they generally go to a lama for a divination or a ritual. The lama first determines the type of spirit bothering the child and then uses barley dough to make an effigy of this spirit. The dough is rubbed all over the child's body, wherever the illness seems to be lodged. In this way, the lama tries to draw out the impressions of the intruding image into the dough. Another piece of dough, reflecting the child's impression, is created and placed near the effigy. This acts as compensation for the effigy and encourages the ghost to leave the child. Rituals are repeated in order to give the effigy life and vitality. Then the lama does a special ritual with the effigy and throws it down on a crossroads so the spirit is taken far away.

This ritual is believed to have significant effects for the child, as when it is carried out to cleanse the infant. Even though the child may not be able to understand what is going on, the parents and everybody around certainly know and begin to act as if the child is normal now that the ritual has been done. Possibly, for some children, it is the "positive thinking" that makes the ritual work. The parent or monk does not enact this ritual in order to enable a child to make friends with the spirit. But it is believed that other positive spirits may be contacted during the ritual, spirits that might aid in subduing the abnormal spirits.

Childhood Rituals

Other cautions and recommendations for the care of young children are given in Norbu Chophel Kharitsang's collection of Tibetan folklore. For example, walking over a child's clothes should be avoided, because it can cause *dip*, the invisible pollution, in the form of a blocked nose and cold. To do this is also considered a sin on the part of the perpetrator. For that matter, children should avoid walking over each other's clothes. If the child is at a walking stage, the *dip* may cause him to trip and fall down frequently because the child's personal deity has been degraded and cannot guide the child properly. Adults may suffer the same repercussions, though to a lesser degree.

There are other general superstitions regarding a child's behavior. It is believed that a child born on the thirtieth day of a month will always be asking for something. Tibetans believe that children are capable of predicting the future and revealing the unknown, quite inadvertently. For instance, sometimes children play warlike games and enjoy them immensely, sometimes winning, sometimes losing, and lurking behind the enemy like real commandos. But the older Tibetans dislike such games, believing they will produce real war or fighting, and so they scold the children. On the other hand, if a child says something auspicious or acts in a very auspicious manner in front of an elderly Tibetan, the child will be rewarded. If a child cries incessantly for no reason whatsoever, it is believed that a visitor from afar will arrive soon. And if a child bends over and looks backward between its legs, the action is believed to indicate that its mother is, or soon will be, pregnant. It is said that the child is looking to see who is following.

Several Tibetan scholars have recorded what they know of traditional Tibetan childcare practices. Thubten Sangay and Norbu Chophel Kharitsang are perhaps the most thorough of these scholars. In a section entitled "Health of the Child" Thubten Sangay states:

> The childcare scriptures say that the child's first birthday should be celebrated by hoisting prayer flags and making the finest offerings to the deities and protectors. The child should be bathed, dressed in new clothes, and taken for an audience with a spiritual master. Afterwards the family dine on the best food and drink and enjoy themselves. [53]

Childhood Illnesses

Thubten Sangay's article in *Tibetan Medicine* also contains information on the Tibetan view regarding the causes of children's illnesses and diseases, along with their diagnoses and treatment. The article lists specific types of illnesses, including teething, diarrhea, measles, and vomiting, which were discussed earlier, in the chapter on infancy. Sangay specifies twenty-four categories of childhood illnesses altogether—which should not be confused with the classification of twenty-four spirit disturbances.

In general there are twenty-four kinds of illnesses affecting children. The conditions for some of them come from the mother and some arise due to improper care of the child. Conditions coming from the mother involve improper care for her health during pregnancy and during breast-feeding. Illnesses or deformities may come about due to the mother contracting some disorder during pregnancy which then befalls the child. These deformities are inborn and hard to cure. Others are more easily cured. For the illnesses which are easy to cure parents should consult a wise doctor at once and follow his instructions exactly. If the baby is being only breastfed, the mother takes all the medicine. If it is both breastfed and eats solids, mother and child share the medicine. A completely weaned baby takes all the medicine. [54]

Special care is given to young children in cases of sickness, accidents, and disabilities—including disabilities from birth, like Down's syndrome or retardation. There doesn't seem to be a great incidence of retardation in Tibet as compared to other countries, but if there is a congenital condition that affects the mind—or a physical condition such as blindness, deafness, or a cleft palate—the treatment always includes ritual. The parents may ask lamas to do a series of religious ceremonies. And the child is nurtured with as much contact as possible since medically there is little, if anything, that can be done. Such a child is still treated as an important part of the family. While parents may wonder about the cause of a condition such as retardation, wondering perhaps if it results from some difficult karma, there is no stigma attached to the condition. And if the child is accepted at home—even if he or she is autistic—then the child stands a much better chance of being accepted by the rest of the community. A child with the solid nurturing of his or her family will go through all the taunting which is ordinary and bound to happen during childhood, but without a destructive or separating effect.

The family responds to an accident immediately with special rituals. If a child has an accident, he or she is laid down, covered, and given some special pills blessed by a lama. Families often keep these blessed pills on hand. It is common for people to keep these blessed pills in their shrine or in their amulet. As these pills are precious and possess protective qualities, many people wear them around their neck. Such pills may even be passed down from generation to generation. Blessed pills are often brought as a present to someone, or they might be used as a temple offering.

When children are sick, they get special attention in the family. If an illness is severe, the parents may take their child to a spiritual master. If the illness is not very severe, or if it is a light fever, the mother will administer blessed herbs or blessed pills and take care of the child herself. Illness warrants everyone's emotional attention and concern. Parents change their work schedules to be with their child, and brothers and sisters might stop going to school in order to help. A doctor will be called in the case of a serious injury or illness.

Children and Their Role in the Family

Right after birth, the child is recognized as part of an extended family. The newest child is considered special, but the main priority is to bind the child into the family and community. Some sibling tensions exist—various things may arouse sibling discord, such as one child's jealousy of another—but these difficulties are seen as normal. As a remedy, parents insist that siblings or friends make up immediately after a disagreement. Children are strongly encouraged to keep harmony. Parents often tell the elder child to give his or her toy, or whatever it was that caused the argument, to the younger child. The focus is not on understanding how each child feels, pacifying the hurt child, or teaching the children to say what they need, as happens in the United States. Rather, the focus is on bringing harmony between the two siblings. This emphasis on harmony and getting along is strong in Eastern cultures, and children learn quickly that giving, rather than competing, is praised. They learn skills and strategies to work out their differences without causing distress to anyone else. In many ways this approach adds continuity and strength to the family, culture, and community.

Such a practice seems fundamentally different from the attitude in Western cultures, which tend to work largely from a different perspective: an individual's feelings come first. The United States was built on the expression of the individual, and most Westerners feel it is important to have their side of the story heard and their feelings and perspective understood before they can work harmoniously with others. This attitude is fostered in childhood as parents try to be fair to all children, considering each perspective equally.

Tenzin Gyatso, the Fourteenth Dalai Lama

Perspective on the Tibetan principle of harmony was given by the Dalai Lama on the day it was announced that he had received the Nobel Peace Prize. In a talk in California, His Holiness said, "First we must investigate through our own daily experience the consequences of anger and the consequences of compassion and love. Then we will be able to come, from our own experience, to a deeper awareness of the negativities of anger and the positiveness of compassion. And once we are inwardly convinced of the goodness of compassion, then we may strengthen it in our lives. Once we realize anger and hatred bring greater unhappiness, then we can be cautious when it arises. When we feel that anger comes as a protector, it can deceive us. It may seem as if anger can provide energy for action. Yet action motivated by anger is not effective. Without anger we can analyze a situation, and then if the situation truly shows that we need strong counteraction, we can do that without ill feeling. Then we have a genuine sense of universal responsibility when we consider the long-term consequences."

Many Tibetan parents today grew up with this attitude toward harmony and strive to pass it on to their children. But since a child younger than eight is not expected to understand the connection between feelings and situations and consequences, the parent often teaches primarily by providing an example for imitation, enforcing rules in accordance with the principle of harmony and limiting the child's exposure to escalating conflict. A Tibetan nun once told me, "Children need discipline and must be given guidance by their parents, who are models for the family and who must help the child deal with attachment and anger. So it is important that parents learn to be content with what they have and be examples of a balanced mind."

In the West, when there is a conflict between siblings, the primary focus may not be that the children must make up right away. In Tibet, it is considered important to bring the children together right away to resolve the situation. Each child learns that creating conflict makes it more likely that what he or she wants will be taken away and given to another child. In Tibet, demanding your own rights is not valued, because it doesn't fit into the concept of being a part of the family. Simply put, in the United States children are treated more as individuals, while in Tibet they are treated as part of a collective. This is an important distinction between the two cultures and it is clearly demonstrated in even the most basic of Tibetan childraising practices.

I asked Dr. Rapgay's mother, Pasang Lhamo, about the use of physical punishment in disciplining children. "Children are not punished at a very young age, while they are breastfeeding," she said. "But by the time they are three or four years old, when they are naughty, or if they misbehave repeatedly, then the parents, usually the father, will punish them by corporal means." In the Tibetan culture, children are taught from a young age that fighting and hurting each other is not good. And if they do not listen, they are disciplined. In his autobiography, the Dalai Lama describes himself as a naughty child and recalls that long switches hung on their Potala study room wall to remind his brother and himself of the consequences of disapproved behavior. In the West, we are beginning to understand what a strong effect physical punishment has on a child. We have learned that corporal punishment may have negative effects, influences a child to either overcontrol or undercontrol expression, and undermines a child's capacity to behave in accord with positive intentions. In the Tibetan culture, physical discipline has always been taken for granted; it is not thought of as violence but is considered necessary for the child's learning.

Teaching values to children begins very early in a child's life in terms of relationships with other siblings and in learning not to kill any life, even insects. From an early age, children are taught to give respect to all life forms. They are not told that it is a sin to kill an insect, for example, because they would not understand the meaning of sin. Instead, a parent might discourage them by saying that the insect's mother would be sad, or might be angry and come back and bite the child. Slowly, the child learns in various ways that killing is not acceptable.

Jamyang Sakya, more popularly known as Dagmokusho, wife of H.H. Jigdal Dagchen Sakya Rinpoche of the Phuntsok Palace lineage, of the Sakya school of Tibetan Buddhism, and co-author of *Princess in the Land of Snows*, told me that even her grandchildren, who were born in the United States, have learned to respect the lives of all sentient beings including insects. She reported that even if they see a dead bug, they will pick it up and while holding it in their palm, recite OM MANE PADME HUM, thus learning to generate compassion at an early age. "We bring up our children in a manner that they are taught to appreciate and respect all sentient beings," she explains. It is a humorous but poignant image: a small child finds a dead fly in the corner of a room, gently picks it up, and administers the Tibetan last rites. The Dalai Lama explains, "Tibetan people regard life, any life, as something very sacred, something holy and important, so even when a small insect is killed, we immediately respond with some feeling of compassion. This remains a force in our society."[55]

When I visited classrooms in Dharamsala and in nearby towns, I saw this attitude of sacred compassion demonstrated repeatedly. Teachers corrected their student's mistakes with no tone of reprimand or judgment. Instead they let them know that one answer was right and another wrong and that the right answer was the one they were after. Children took the correction without any sense of humiliation, wrongdoing, or need to act out. There was no teasing by classmates. It seemed simply to be an understood redirection in the path of learning.

There may be occasional physical reprimanding of the child in the classroom. Teachers will sometimes rap their students lightly on the head with a long stick—although it's really more symbolic than painful. Certain qualities are most valued in a child and promoted: compassion, honesty, goodheartedness, sharing. Many children from a young age naturally share things, and soon other children learn that showing these highly prized qualities draws the most positive attention. And before long, this positive behavior happens instinctively. These qualities are emphasized throughout a Tibetan's life.

At a very early age, a child learns where the shrine room is in the family home and learns the proper behavior in this room; he or she must do a prostration upon entering and must at all times be respectful. The focus here, as in all things, is on instilling values and ethics. These are among the first lessons a child learns. And it is important that these lessons be taught spontaneously. When a child does something wrong, it is seen as an opportunity to teach the child. The teaching happens as life happens; evaluating and teaching a child takes place all the time as a natural process.

Tibetan children are brought up to believe in the sacredness and spiritual nature of the family. Each family has a rich history, and Tibetans feel a responsibility to continue a lineage from one generation to another. In a more spiritual sense, a child realizes that being born into a family is a small part of the vast cycle of rebirth that is an important part of the Tibetans' spiritual practice. Family is one vehicle for spiritual growth as a child can explore the inner dynamics of the family and discover the essence of what a family is like. This becomes a valuable tool in spiritual practice, which also links experience with intellect. Spiritual competence later on is strengthened by participation, heightened awareness, and direct experience in this family process. In this sense, the spiritual bonds between family and child are very important. Such bonding may also take a more physical form. A Tibetan child often sleeps with his or her parents, right up to the age of five or seven. In particular, the child spends a great deal of time with his or her mother. Even during work, a mother is hesitant to leave her child and will often carry him or her on her back up to the age of four.

In the West, perhaps due to the stressing of individual strengths, there seems to be a tendency for a baby to begin toddling earlier than in the East. In the East parents tend to keep babies more protected and to carry them longer. In the West, verbal language also seems to be learned much more quickly—perhaps because, in the East, a very young child usually associates primarily with his or her mother and extended family, where body rhythms and intuitions are exchanged beyond words. Traditionally, Tibetans believe that a child is very vulnerable in this early time, so a child is protected and is not exposed to strangers until the child is at least a year old. However, this tendency is changing. Tibetans in Dharamsala and the younger generation of parents there are much more open to people than their ancestors and allow their children much more contact outside of the family.

Tibetan Education

When a child is around seven years old, traditionally there were two basic options for education. Children could go to a local lay school, where they learned basic skills: how to read and write and, maybe when they were older, grammar and a bit of poetry. However, the best academic training was found in the monasteries or the nunneries, which contributed to the choice of one-fifth or one-sixth of the male population to become monks. Traditionally, a household would "donate" one son to the local monastery, although that practice is not so regularly followed anymore. Girls were sometimes "donated" to a nunnery, though there were, and still are, fewer nunneries than monasteries. Studies at the monastery were not, and are not currently, confined to spiritual topics. Initially, classes are primarily spiritual or classical, focusing in the early years on repetition and memorization of mantra and text. Soon the lamas include literature, poetry, grammar, medicine, art, and astrology. While higher education for Tibetans formerly was dominated by the monasteries, many young exiled Tibetans pursue degrees in universities and colleges where they now live.

The present monastic education is fundamentally the same as it has been for thousands of years. There are a few monasteries in South India that are centers for Tibetan learning and one institute in Varanasi that educates both lay and monastic students. To some extent, a Tibetan monastery education in India is very similar to traditional education in Tibet; in fact, many of the teachers are from Tibetan monasteries. But it is also different in fundamental ways. For instance, laypeople and monks now study in the same classroom. And Tibetan students must conform in some ways to the Indian academic curriculum, such as by earning a bachelor's degree or master's degree and by learning an additional and more standard curriculum, including Hindi, English, Sanskrit, mathematics, and science.

There are schools in each of the Tibetan communities in India and several schools in Dharamsala. The children are generally taught Tibetan, English, reading, writing, math, art, and music, with the workload becoming increasingly rigorous as they grow older and advance to higher grades. The younger children have many games and songs and spend only twenty or so minutes at a time learning letters and numbers at their slates. Each year they are expected to do more work until they can accommodate a full academic load.

An important issue related to family unity is the concern when Tibetan children break away from the family in order to go away to study. This is an increasingly important issue as more and more Tibetans have access to schools in other parts of the world. The choice about each child's schooling must address the struggle to balance the values of maintaining Tibetan culture with integrating one's life into the rest of the world. Leaving home to go to school is often rationalized as a necessity. But essentially, perhaps unconsciously, it is also an act of breaking away from the family and its traditions. There is often compensatory reasoning applied to the move, rationalizing that the children may send money home when they have established a career after their schooling. Nonetheless, it often breaks up the family and in many ways erodes long-standing cultural traditions. In many cases, children are only in touch through the exchange of money, financial support, or letters which affirm some emotional bonding. By the time the student is old enough and financially stable enough to go back and visit, the parents may already have passed away. So while going away to school may have the advantages of a good education, there may also be tragic consequences in the resulting family and cultural discontinuity.

In a Tibetan Schoolroom

To research the Tibetan school system firsthand, I visited Dorje's older sister, Paldon, a cheerful middle-aged Tibetan woman who was a teacher in Dharamsala. It was clear from the start that the children obviously adored her, and they gave her copious hugs throughout a day of games and writing exercises. I was impressed by the easy balance Paldon maintained in her classroom with six and seven year-olds, giving warm affection and reassuring touches to the children while at the same time expressing control and authority in the class. The children were also affectionate with one another, putting their arms around one another during exercises or game instructions.

Paldon worked mostly from imagination and memory, referring periodically to what the children called "teacher's book" in which lessons and exercises from her teaching training were recorded. This was the only text available to the class and the children recognized it as a prized item, not even daring to touch it. Schools have little money for resources so each teacher has to hand write his or her own training guide. Consequently, Paldon was eager to exchange curriculum ideas with me and laboriously copied songs I taught the children into her book. Paldon was open and responsive to the children and took delight in the capabilities of each student. She knew just how long to spend on each activity and lost no time as she smoothly flowed from one exercise to the next with no dead spaces to breed boredom or restlessness. The games were punctuated by laughter. She created an atmosphere in which it was fun to learn.

In a favorite game, a student put small blocks with English letters face down on the floor, listened to the teacher whisper the letter sound in his or her ear, then carefully peeked at each letter to select the proper one for that sound. Another game involved Paldon mixing up the textured letter blocks and holding one in front of a child who, without looking, must trace the letter with a finger and say which letter he or she had touched. I watched as each one did this exercise carefully and successfully, time after time. If they were not successful, Paldon was not punitive. She simply corrected the child, who smiled and accepted the correction. The children had great fun in learning the games and I witnessed very little problem with discipline.

Janet Ryan Richardson, a social psychologist from California, researched children's spirituality in Tibetan cultures. Much of her research was based in and near Dharamsala. Janet explained to me that many of the Tibetan schools in India were based on the Montessori model. Maria Montessori taught in India earlier in the century and her educational model has been widely adapted throughout India. Many of the Tibetan schools I visited had signs that indicated they were Montessori Schools and that they had been aided by European or North American groups such as Save the Children. These schools had a smattering of well-used Montessori learning tools, either purchased in Indian cities or donated from Europe or North America. In Paldon's school they had a small collection of long, narrow boards with English words on them; a box of small three-inch squares of wood to sort colors; a box that made different sounds; and a collection of textured boards, stencils, variously shaped wooden pieces, and building blocks.

With the few resources available, they worked creatively and enthusiastically. "The children take delight in little games," Janet told me, "like putting the boards with the words on their heads and then guessing the words. These schools cannot even afford books and children write on slates with tiny, thin pieces of chalk. But the children laughed a lot, as did the teachers. There is a strong sense of joy—the same feeling I saw in the

Tibetan Children's Village, a community for orphans and children whose families cannot support them."

In Tibet, Janet had expected to find poor children in understaffed and underfunded schools. This was true in a material sense, but she also found a profound sense of joy and love throughout Tibetan schools, a feeling that she wanted to carry back with her into the U.S. school environment. "It isn't the very sober atmosphere we find in U.S. schools," Janet said. "We Americans take ourselves so seriously. We believe there is a time to play and a time to work and create such separation in our lives. I don't see this separation between work and play, or the secular and the spiritual, in Tibetan children. They are very integrated children."

These children, unlike the young monks and nuns, were not expected to sit for hours of continuous learning but moved from one task to another while their minds were still fresh and curious. The change of activities flowed easily and smoothly through the whole school day, and these activities included a break when they went home for lunch, games and songs, and writing letters on their slates. In the schools Janet and I visited, we both found a balance between school and family time, with children moving naturally and easily between the two.

Tibetans prize memorization, believing that a text is not really known until it is committed to memory. Only then can one truly analyze and critique the literature. I have often seen young monks and nuns sitting for hours and hours chanting pages of their books to themselves. As lay children grow older, they, too, are introduced to massive amounts of memorization. Paldon told me that most lessons to be memorized are spoken out loud so the students can hear them and feel the vibrations and rhythms the sounds make. Teachers give the lessons in flowing cadences so the students can easily chant and remember them.

Once while visiting a monastery a few hours away from Dharamsala, I heard chanting emanating from a room on the side of the monastery and peeked in to see an older monk slouched in a chair at the head of the room patiently repeating lessons to young monks who chanted as loud as they could. It was as if the stronger a voice they could give to each lesson, the more they could demonstrate the sincerity of their scholarship to the teacher. While visiting the Center School for Tibetans in Dalhousie, a school for Tibetans started by the Indian government, I walked by a huge study hall one night and heard a cacophony of voices chanting lessons louder and louder. In the United States one imagines a study hall to be a big room of silent students working autonomously on their homework. In Tibetan schools, the louder the group recitation, the more orderly the study hall.

The Tibetan Children's Village

The Tibetan Children's Village has been active for over thirty years and has branches throughout the Tibetan refugee settlements. It houses and educates more than six thousand children, about fifteen hundred of them in Dharamsala.[56] This efficient school for refugee orphans, once directed by the Dalai Lama's oldest sister, Tsering Dolma, is a beautiful village tucked on the mountainside. (Mrs. Pema Gyalpo, the Dalai Lama's younger sister, is the current head of the Tibetan Children's Village.) I was particularly impressed by how the Tibetan Children's Village is not just a school, but a whole village. People of all ages live there. Children stay in bunk rooms and are looked after by houseparents. The children have relationships with people of all ages, grandparents, aunts, uncles, brothers, and sisters: it's truly like a big family. The Tibetan Children's Village is an inspiring model for other refugee communities that are trying to provide sound education and care for their children. Any refugee population has the challenge of preparing their children for the host country in which they find themselves, while at the same time implanting in the children their own traditional cultural heritage. The Tibetan Children's Village has been able to expose the children to both worlds.

After the Chinese military invaded Tibet, many children came with their families over the mountain passes to India. Some of these children died on the journey. And many more children died in India, often because Tibetans didn't know how to protect their children from the diseases picked up in a new country. They began to cast about for ideas to help solve this problem. At first, in the early 1960s, a number of Tibetan children were adopted by Westerners with the thought of providing them with a comfortable life. But the Tibetans didn't have experience with the

Western aspects of life and therefore had a lot of trouble assimilating to a very different lifestyle. As these children grew up, some committed suicide, and a disproportionate number of them became involved with drugs and violence as they unsuccessfully tried to maintain both their adopted and genetic cultures simultaneously. The children who adapted well were assimilated so heavily into European culture that they lost their sense of being Tibetan. This was a real blow to the Tibetan community because these children were the hope for the future of Tibet. The community was desperate to pull something together, to find a way or an organization to provide for the children's needs and still enable them to retain their link to the Tibetan culture.

Coming from a strong academic background, the Tibetan people researched models from all over the world to explore how they could care for and educate their children and allow them to retain their traditional culture. Tibetans have valued learning from other cultures throughout their history. In the seventh century C.E. when the Tibetan king Songtsen Gampo decided to create a written alphabet for their language, he sent his learned minister Thonmi Sambhota to India to find models that other countries had used. Choosing to adapt a Sanskrit script, he created the structure and characters for a written Tibetan alphabet. This sort of scholarship and research of other models is seen in the development of other aspects of the culture, both historical and contemporary. Tibetan medicine, for example, also developed through a series of conferences, from as early as the third century, which included Indian, Chinese, Persian, Egyptian, and Greek scholars and healers. Currently, the Tibetan government in exile, under the direction of the Dalai Lama, is studying examples from countries all over the world as it considers revisions to its constitution for democracy.

For the care of children without families, the Dalai Lama and his government eventually decided to use the model of the SOS Kinderdorf International in Vienna, Austria. The Dalai Lama gave funding and direction to the project, and a number of Westerners committed crucial funds to help start and continue the village and its affiliates in other refugee settlements over the years. It is impressive to see that children can be successfully raised with a sense of purpose that permeates their education as well as their community. In the Tibetan Children's Village, the primary goals are to provide orphans and underprivileged Tibetan children with warmth and love, to give these children a solid education that will prepare them for both the outside world and for Tibet when it is free again, and to instill in the children their strong Tibetan heritage.

Janet told me that the adults she met at the Tibetan Children's Village were determined that the children experience Tibetan culture, especially Tibetan family culture. "It wasn't that these orphans and refugee children were to be pitied and pawned off on whomever could raise them. In fact, a delightful family structure was set up. I couldn't have hoped for a better one for any child."

The Dalai Lama wrote about the origins of the Village in the Twenty-fifth Anniversary Silver Jubilee information brochure for the Tibetan Children's Village: "When tragedy befell Tibet in 1959, among the many Tibetans who escaped to neighboring India was a large number of children. Owing to our lack of experience in providing necessary and proper healthcare, the lives of many of these children were endangered. The Nursery for Tibetan Children was established in Dharamsala in 1960 to meet the special and urgent needs of the children at the time. Gradually, through much effort, improvement in the facilities was achieved, provision of education to the children was introduced, and the institution began to expand. The name changed to Tibetan Children's Village. Since that time the institution has provided succor and education, both traditional and modern, to over seven thousand Tibetan children."

Tibetans in India must maintain a delicate balance to keep up with a world from which they have been so isolated for many centuries, and, at the same time, to keep their Tibetan identities and the dignity of their heritage. They, and the institutions they create, such as the Tibetan Children's Village, are inspirations for all of us who strive to find a balance of old and new in our own lives.

A grandmother carries her grandchild in the traditional manner.

Epilogue: Learnings from a Tibetan Heritage

Gathering

As I prepared to leave Dharamsala and my friends, I tried to bring together all the information I had gathered on Tibetan birth ways and find ways to present the information so that both non-Tibetans and Tibetans could use it effectively and beneficially. I was grateful for the understanding of Tibetan culture that I had received from so many warm and gracious teachers. And I knew I would miss my morning circumambulation, easy afternoons of talk and tea with Palmo and Tsering, and long discussions into the night with the families of all my friends. I didn't know when I would be able to make my way back into their welcoming homes again. Slowly, I began to say good-bye, a process which took several days, as good-byes meant long, meaningful afternoons together, or even full days of special outings and farewell dinners. It was a wonderful time as it intensified and solidified our friendships and deepened my commitment to share what they had taught me of their ways of birth and childcare.

On my last morning visit with Gyatso, I asked him to tell me what he would like me to write about, what he considered the most important lessons about birth in the Tibetan culture from which others could benefit. I asked, "If you could raise a child in an ideal way, so that it would be the best world citizen it could be, what would you do? If you were to recommend the most important ideas from Tibetan childraising practices to Westerners, what would they be?" As usual, he thought very seriously about the question before replying, but his answer was definite: "The most important aspect of Tibetan birth for people in other cultures to know is the value and use of spiritual ritual and initiations. When the baby smiles for the first time, celebrate it. When the baby walks for the first time, that is significant. Write it down. Capture the magic and celebration of each new development in an infant's life. Massage and bodily touch from the moment of birth are also essential to full development. And breastfeeding needs to happen as soon after birth as possible."

Gyatso also mentioned the need to preserve the Tibetan heritage. "We need to preserve the Tibetan heritage for our own children and families. The most important values for people in our culture are wisdom and compassion, respect for the continuity of all life, the rituals to mark consciousness, and the ways of teaching children. Collectively, Tibet can become a free land again where people live in peace and harmony with their environment. If we do not succeed, in the next twenty to thirty years most Tibetans will be assimilated and married to others. Those who are in America for example would likely become more Americanized. Those in Switzerland would become more Swiss. And much of the culture of their children would then come from the traditions of their new homelands. Much would be lost."

As he spoke, Gyatso and I arrived at the temple room that housed the large prayer wheel Gyatso and I were in the habit of spinning together. Each day we added a new prayer. "Today we will pray for your safe journey home," he announced as he took one side of the wheel. I took the other side, and we began to walk round and round. The bell suspended from the ceiling announced each completed round, ringing as it hit the metal prong that extended from the side of the big cylinder. I did, indeed, feel my journey home would be safe with the power of these prayers. Gyatso and I circled again and again, putting our concentration and strength into pushing the prayer wheel until it whirled and spoke on its own momentum, sending the prayers embossed on the sides of the large cylinder out into the universe.

Reflections

In writing this book, many memories of my friends and experiences in Tibet have come easily to the surface. For instance, the other day I heard a church bell in the distance and for a moment thought it was a gong at the monastery in Dharamsala. I could practically hear the rhythmic thud of Gyatso's leather boots, feel Palmo's warm eyes and touch as she invited me to stay for one of her delicious *mo-mo* or thugpa dinners and listen to Rinchen Lhamo relive her early days in Tibet as she reminisced about her midwifery experiences. The morning's mail the other day brought a letter from Lhamo with a recent picture of Dolma Tsering, who was already a toddler. Lhamo had been so sure this child was going to be a daughter, and I had never doubted her certainty. Still, I'll never forget the huge grin on her face when she told me that indeed, her new baby was a girl. So many hopes and dreams have been placed in the children of Tibetan cultures, both within Tibet and in exile.

I've also found myself reflecting more and more on the Dalai Lama's dream of peace. The week before I had left for the Himalayas, I was in California at a conference, Harmonia Mundi, with the Dalai Lama. It was then that the announcement came, suddenly and with little forewarning, that he had received the 1989 Nobel Peace Prize. In Dharamsala, I was told, many Tibetans did not know what the Nobel Peace Prize was or its significance in the world's perception, but the word quickly spread and the entire town became caught up in jubilant celebration. For the next few days, Tibetans celebrated nonstop. Shops were closed, doors opened, and neighbors and visitors danced together in the streets. After thirty years in exile, after all the struggle and hard work they had gone through, these people were exuberant that their leader had received world recognition.

"Indians, Tibetans, and Westerners all drank from the same glass," one exhilarated Tibetan shopkeeper told me. "It was an incredible time. People danced and danced, for three whole days, all through the streets." Families went on picnics in droves, a favorite pastime of Tibetans. Special food was prepared, baskets were filled with delicacies, and whole groups of people headed into the forests and to other favorite places to celebrate. The Dalai Lama's Nobel Peace Prize gave hope to many Tibetans that all their efforts to survive with cultural integrity would pay off. It gave them a sense that they hadn't been forgotten by the world and that anything was possible, that the Chinese could go home and leave their country free for them once again.

In this book I hope to bring another part of Tibetan wisdom to the attention of the world. My time with Palmo and Ngawang, Tsering and Tashi, Lhamo and Dorje, their families, and all my other Tibetan friends, has shown me much about the relationship between birth, life, and death. I have learned how the Tibetan culture celebrates the continuum that runs through the seven stages of birth. I have been fortunate to find a culture that integrates the birth process from preconception through early childhood; provides an earthy and spacious family, community, and universal context; and simply and naturally includes body, emotions, mind, spirit, environment and relationships in its practical approach to living, life after life. The Dalai Lama and all Tibetans have myriad gifts to offer the world. I join them in prayers that they may soon return home to live in peace. The Dalai Lama's vision is for Tibet to become an international environmental preserve. Let us work together toward that goal, and until then, let us learn from the wisdom they share with us while maintaining their culture and heritage in exile.

Acknowledgments

Eight Tibetan scholars read our first draft in 1991 and 1992, fine-tuning its cultural, medical, and religious accuracy. We thank Norbu Chophel Kharitsang, writer and scholar of Tibetan folklore at the Tibetan Library of Works and Archives in Dharamsala, India (now in Madison, Wisconsin, in the United States); Lama Ngawang Jorden, lama in the Sakya tradition and scholar at Harvard University; Venerable Dugu Choegyal Rinpoche, Tashi Jong Tibetan Community, head of Kham · Chamdo Tho-Dugu Monastery, president of Dugu Vajrayana Heritage Foundation, and founder of the Tara Bhir Tho-Dugu Retreat Center in Kathmandu, Nepal; Joanna Macy, Ph.D., of Berkeley, California, who is a writer, professor, and scholar in Tibetan religion and philosophy; Jamyang Sakya, of Seattle, Washington, who is the author of *Princess in the Land of Snows* (Boston: Shambhala Publications, 1990), cofounder of the Sakya Center in Seattle, and the first Tibetan refugee to give birth in the United States (in 1961); Dr. Lobsang Rapgay, doctor of Tibetan medicine and Ph.D. in psychology; Mark Tatz, Ph.D., scholar and professor of Tibetan culture, philosophy, and language; and Kevin Ergil, Ph.D., Tibetologist, medical anthropologist, physician of traditional Chinese medicine, and student of Tibetan medicine. We are grateful to all for their contributions, detailed information, scholarship, and encouragement.

Additional thanks to Norbu Chophel Kharitsang, Ngawang Jorden, Lobsang Rapgay, Jamyang Sakya, and Mark Tatz for re-reading the final draft in 1997, and final editing for details of cultural and religious specifics. Our thanks to Don Brown, M.D., a founder of the Kadampa Center for the Practice of Tibetan Buddhism, in Raleigh, North Carolina, who took the work to Timothy McNeill of Wisdom Publications, and also commented on the final draft.

Susanna Ralli, freelance editor for Wisdom Publications, reshaped and trimmed the manuscript with extraordinary sensitivity to the authors' intentions and the reader's needs. Constance Miller, Stephanie Shaiman, and Sara McClintock at Wisdom Publications asked and answered questions with consistent probing and valued encouragement.

Other readers who gave invaluable comments and support include Hank Maiden—who contributed to the book's concept and design, and copyedited drafts over many years—Tsewang Tatz, Adriana Rocco, Eric Maisel, and Jay Mead. Thanks to Jay especially for childcare. We thank Janet Ryan Richardson for sharing her research on children's education in Dharamsala and her photographs. Additional thanks to Susan Lirikas Nicolay, Amina Tirana, and Thomas L. Kelly for their photographs. Special thanks to Lama Ngawang Jorden for many years of friendship, scholarly information, and translations.

We are grateful to His Holiness the Dalai Lama, Pasang Lhamo, Dr. Yeshe Dhonden, and innumerable other Tibetans who patiently answered questions. And we are especially grateful to Tsomo and Norbu Chophel Kharitsang for their friendship and interest in the project; for their detailed information, editing, and advice; for arranging interviews in Dharamsala; and for the timely arrival of their youngest daughter, Dolkar Tsering. Additional gratitude is given to the nuns at Tilokpur Mahayana Buddhist Nunnery for their hospitality, Buddhist scholarship, cultural anecdotes, and gift of a Green Tara tanka.

We express appreciation as well to Angeles Arrien, Peter Beren, George Churinoff, Mary Davenport, Lisa Faithorn, Carol Ferraro, Djann Hoffman, Lisa Mackinney, Gladys McGarey, Jonathan Nelson, Helena Norberg-Hodge, Michael Phillips, Gangchen Rinpoche, Leslie Rossman, Mark Salzwedel, Ellen Weis, and Gordon Whiting for valued support and consultation; to Elisa Odabashian for early editorial contributions; and to Rebecca Rothfusz for initial editing and indexing ideas.

We would also like to express our deep gratitude to Rinchen Khando Choegyel, Minister of Education for the Tibetan Government in Exile, and Director of the Tibetan Nun's Project in Dharamsala, for providing such a thoughtful preface to this volume. Her deep love and admiration for the men, women, and children of Tibet is a great source of inspiration and joy. May her aspirations for her people be quickly fulfilled.

Anne Hubbell Maiden
Berkeley, CA
June 1997

Edie Farwell
San Francisco, California
June 1997

Appendix

Organizations Working on Behalf of Tibetan Women and Children and a Free Tibet

TIBETAN WOMEN'S ASSOCIATION (TWA)
Bhagsunag Road
P.O. McLeod Ganj 176219
Dharamsala, District Kangra. HP. India
Tel: 91-1892-22527
Fax: 91-1892-23374 or 22589
E-mail: twa@cta.unv.ernet.in
Sponsors broad-based cultural, political, and charitable projects.

TIBETAN CHILDREN'S VILLAGE (TCV)
Dharamsala Cantt. 176 216 HP. India
Tel: 91-1892-23348 or 23354
Fax: 91-1892-22670
Houses and educates orphaned and needy Tibetan children.

INTERNATIONAL CAMPAIGN FOR TIBET (ICT)
1735 Eye Street, NW, Suite 615
Washington, DC 20006
Tel: 202-785-1515
Fax: 202-785-4343
E-mail: ict@peacenet.org
URL: http://www.peacenet.org/ict
Promotes human rights and democratic freedom in Tibet.

For a thorough list of organizations, contact the International Campaign for Tibet at the address above for the most recent edition of their *International Tibet Resource Directory*.

Notes

1. *The Tibetan Book of the Dead*, as translated by Francesca Fremantle and Chogyam Trungpa (Boston: Shambhala Press, 1987), and *Death, Intermediate State and Rebirth* by Lati Rinbochay and Jeffrey Hopkins (Ithaca: Snow Lion, 1979).

2. It is important to note that this is a layperson's introduction to Tibetan birth practices. Far more information is known, such as how to guide the process of reincarnation, which rests on advanced Tibetan Buddhist teaching, practice, and initiations.

3. From a Cherokee medicine teaching. See Dhyani Ywahoo, *Voices of Our Ancestors: Cherokee Teachings from the Wisdom Fire* (Boston: Shambhala, 1987), 268.

4. The Dalai Lama and Galen Rowell, *My Tibet* (Berkeley: University of California Press, 1990), 27.

5. It is hard to get exact figures for both Tibetan and Chinese populations in Tibet because what is currently called the Tibetan Autonomous Region does not include Kham and Amdo, the two most populous provinces of historical Tibet. For a detailed look at population transfer numbers, see Warren Smith's *Tibetan Nation* (Colorado: Westview Press, 1996). As of November 1996, approximately 130,000 Tibetans live in exile.

6. The text of the Dalai Lama's five-point peace plan is included in the anthology, *The Anguish of Tibet*, edited by Petra Kelly, Gert Bastian, and Pat Aiello (Berkeley: Parallax Press, 1991).

7. Per an eleventh-century Tibetan text, whose title is translated as *Illustrated Principles and Practices of Tibetan Medicine*.

8. The Dalai Lama and Galen Rowell, *My Tibet*, 79.

9. Ibid., 30.

10. The hope that children will carry on the traditions of a culture that is threatened by genocide or disaster is mirrored in stories of indigenous people and refugees on nearly all continents. From early times, Tibetans have sought learning from other cultures and have also recognized that creating opportunities to teach what they have learned, wherever they are, is one way to keep their culture alive.

11. References to Dr. Dolma's writings in this and subsequent chapters are from the chapter "Child Conception," in *Lectures on Tibetan Medicine* (New Delhi, India: Library of Tibetan Works and Archives, 1986), 83–117.

12. From an article by photojournalist Catherine Alport, "Crossing Cultures with Women," *Women of Power*, Summer 1987.

13. See *The Cult of Tara: Magic and Ritual in Tibet* (Berkeley: University of California Press, 1978) by Stephan Beyer for a more thorough description of Tara in Tibetan Buddhism.

14. This account is found in Lati Rinbochay and Jeffrey Hopkins's *Death, Intermediate State and Rebirth* (Ithaca, New York: Snow Lion, 1979), 29. This is a translation of the *Lamp Thoroughly Illuminating the Presentation of the Three Basic Bodies—Death, Intermediate State and Rebirth* by Yang-jen-ga-way-lo-dro, an eighteenth-century scholar and yogi of the Gelugpa order.

15. From an interview with Tibetologist Kevin Ergil, in 1990. Dr. Ergil, former President of the American College of Traditional Chinese Medicine in San Francisco, trained as a medical anthropologist and studied under Dr. Yeshe Dhonden in Dharamsala.

16. See *The Tibetan Book of the Dead* for a complete discussion of the bardo. We were most often referred to the version edited by Francesca Freemantle and Chögyam Trungpa (Boston: Shambhala, 1987). Robert Thurman has since made another vigorous translation (New York: Bantam, 1994).

17. For a fuller explanation of transitions in the intermediate state, see the preface to *Death, Intermediate State and Rebirth*, by Lati Rinbochay and Jeffrey Hopkins (Ithaca, New York: Snow Lion, 1979), 14–20.

18. From *The Tibetan Book of the Dead*, translated by Francesca Fremantle and Chögyam Trungpa (Boston: Shambhala, 1987), 91–92.

19. *The Ambrosia Heart Tantra*, vol. 1, annotated by Dr. Yeshe Dhonden and translated by Jhampa Kelsang (Dharamsala, India: Library of Tibetan Works and Archives, 1977), 32.

20. "The principal idea of health in Tibetan medicine is that of balance, balance within the body, and between it and its corresponding aspects in the outer world. In terms of the body, that balance is primarily expressed as the harmony of the three humors—wind, bile, and phlegm.

   "The three humors originate on a spiritual plane from the basic mental confusion that produces subject-object dualism and thus the karmic force to manifest life and the universe. Ignorance, desire, and aversion evolve into the humors phlegm, wind, and bile respectively. Once produced, the balanced circulation of these humors on their own course maintains the health of the organism. The three humors are the principle triad in Tibetan somatic medicine." Terry Clifford, in *Tibetan Buddhist Medicine and Psychiatry* (Maine: Samuel Weiser, 1984), 90.

21. Information from Dr. Dhonden in this and subsequent chapters is derived from his two articles "Embryology in Tibetan Medicine" and "Childbirth in Tibetan Medicine," his books *Health Through Balance* and *The Ambrosia Heart Tantra*, and a meeting with him in California.

22. Dr. Yeshe Dhonden's "Embryology in Tibetan Medicine" and "Childbirth in Tibetan Medicine" can be found in *Tibetan Medicine*, no. 1 (Dharamsala, India: Library of Tibetan Works and Archives, 1980).

23. *The Ambrosia Heart Tantra*, 32.

24. Ibid., 31–32.

25. Rinchen Dolma Taring, *Daughter of Tibet* (India: Allied Publishers, 1970), 112.

26. Personal communication with authors, 1989.

27. For more detail, see Sogyal Rinpoche's *The Tibetan Book of Living and Dying* (San Francisco: Harper, 1992), 386–89. Another valued reference for prayers is Geshe Rabten and Geshe Ngawang Dhargyey's *Advice from a Spiritual Friend: Buddhist Thought Transformation* (London: Wisdom Publications, 1984).

28. See Michel Odent's *Primal Health* (London: Century Hutchison, 1986).

29. The text has not been translated into English. The Tibetan title translates as *Illustrated Principles and Practices of Tibetan Medicine*. Information from this text was obtained by Anne in meetings with a Tibetan doctor, Lobsang Rapgay, in San Francisco. He had borrowed a copy of the text, and told Anne Maiden that this was the most thorough traditional Tibetan text on pregnancy and childbirth. They spent hours going over each of the thirty-nine paintings of the birth process as he translated the text accompanying each one. The text was a replica of the original eleventh-century text that

was first printed in Tibet. The few replicated texts in the world that survive are still used by Tibetans studying medicine. Since those meetings, a later work from the seventeenth century that builds upon the earlier text, *Tibetan Medical Paintings: Illustrations to the Blue Beryl Treatise of Sangye Gyamtso (1653–1705)*, has been translated and published in two large volumes, one with full-color plates and commentary, the other with text. It was edited by Yuri Parfionovitch, Gyurme Dorje, and Fernand Meyer, with a foreword by the Dalai Lama (New York: Harry N. Abrams, 1993). Currently out of print, it includes, in one large painting, seventy-eight illustrations of human embryology in the development of the organism. Captions on the painting are in Tibetan, and a facing page includes their translation (pages 181–82). A footnote to the commentary traces the general lineage of this medical teaching, and clarifies its relationship to the eleventh-century text. Beginning in the eighth century, "it continues through the great treasure-finder Trapa Ngonshe (1012–1089), who reputedly rediscovered the texts concealed by Padmasambhava at Samye. He then transmitted their tradition in succession through Darma Trakpei Gyeltsen, Konchok Kyab of Lhartse, Yonten Gonpo the younger (fl. twelfth century), who is revered as the thirteenth incarnation of Yuthog the elder (fl. eighth century), Sumton Chenpo Yeshezung of Nyemo…and their followers" (p.25). There seems to be substantial agreement between the eleventh-century and seventeenth-century versions, with a few additions in the later account.

30. Information from Namkhai Norbu in this and subsequent chapters is from his small monograph *On Birth and Life* (Venice, Italy: Tipografia Commerciale Venezia, 1983), 15–30.

31. Dr. Dolma's information in this section on the thirty-nine weeks of gestation comes from *Lectures on Tibetan Medicine* (New Delhi, India: Library of Tibetan Works and Archives, 1986), 92–103.

32. Western psychologists could consider such a prebirth differentiation as the genesis of individuation.

33. The folktales, superstitions, and customs in this section are from Norbu Chophel Kharitsang's chapter "Tibetan Superstitions Regarding Childbirth," in *Tibetan Medicine*, no. 7 (New Delhi, India, Library of Tibetan Works and Archives, 1984), 25–29.

34. See Geshe Ngawang Dhargyey's *Tibetan Tradition of Mental Development* (New Delhi, India: Library of Tibetan Works and Archives, 1974), 14–20, for a further account of the queen's dream and the life of her son, Buddha Shakyamuni.

35. Vicki MacKenzie, *Reincarnation: The Boy Lama* (Boston: Wisdom Publications, 1996), 91–92.

36. Unsigned news article. "Zong Rinpoche's Incarnation Discovered." *Tibetan Review* (June 1990), 11.

37. The Dalai Lama, *My Land and My People* (New York: McGraw-Hill, 1962), 21–22.

38. A wonderful description of these tests, as well as the Dalai Lama's early life, can be found in *My Land and My People*.

39. The superstitions, customs, and folktales in this chapter are from Norbu Chophel Kharitsang's and Thubten Sangay's articles in *Tibetan Medicine*, no. 7 (1984), 3–29.

40. Lake Manasarovar, a sacred lake in southwestern Tibet, is an important place of pilgrimage for devout Tibetans and Indians.

41. For a thorough explanation of the effects of alcohol taken during pregnancy, see Michael Dorris's *The Broken Cord* (New York: Harper & Row, 1989).

42. There was strong dissonance within Tibetan school children when the Chinese launched campaigns to kill flies and other creatures.

43. Thubten Sangay's "Tibetan Traditions of Childbirth and Childcare," in *Tibetan Medicine* (1984), 13. The notes to this article (pages 22–24) contain a discussion of the ingredients for preparing a number of Tibetan medicines.

44. Ibid., 13.

45. References to traditional customs in pre-Chinese-invasion Tibet in this section are from assorted sections of *Daughter of Tibet*, by Rinchen Dolma Taring (London: Wisdom Publications, 1986.)

46. Childcare customs in this section are from Norbu Chophel Kharitsang's *Folk Cultures of Tibet* (New Delhi, India: Library of Tibetan Works and Archives, 1983).

47. See Yeshe Dhonden, *Health Through Balance* (Ithaca, New York: Snow Lion, 1986) and Terry Clifford, *Tibetan Buddhist Medicine and Psychiatry* (Maine: Samuel Weiser, 1984). Briefly, "hot" illnesses are likened to fire, are located in the lower body, and are associated with dryness and rising. These illnesses are characterized by fevers, inflammations, and upper body aches, including headaches or digestive pain. "Cold" maladies are likened to water and earth, are located in the upper body, and are associated with moisture and dampness and descending through the body. They are characterized by coldness and heaviness in mind and body, loss of appetite and taste, belching, and vomiting. For a cold disorder it is recommended to sit by the fire or in the sun and to wear warm clothing. For a hot dysfunction,

one would eat cool food, like yogurt, and sit by the seashore, along with other treatments. The aim is balance throughout the system.

48. Thubten Sangay, "Tibetan Traditions of Childbirth and Childcare," *Tibetan Medicine* (1984), 17.

49. Ibid., 19.

50. Ibid., 12–13.

51. The pictures and images described in this section are from the *Illustrated Principles and Practices of Tibetan Medicine*. These illustrations are not included in the recent edition of *Tibetan Medical Paintings: Illustrations to the Blue Beryl Treatise of Sangye Gyamtso (1653–1705)*, (New York: Harry N. Abrams, 1993).

52. Thubten Sangay, "Tibetan Traditions of Childbirth and Childcare," 14.

53. Ibid., 12–13.

54. Ibid., 14.

55. The Dalai Lama, *My Tibet*, 72.

56. Most of the initial funding was provided by the Indian Government. Now SOS International meets much of the expense.

Glossary

Avalokiteshvara (Sanskrit): The name of the bodhisattva of compassion. In Tibetan, Chenrezig. His Holiness the Fourteenth Dalai Lama is felt to be an incarnation of this deity.

bardo (Tibetan): The state into which one goes immediately after death, where one remains until taking rebirth. The intermediate state between death and rebirth; literally, the in-between.

bodhisattva (Sanskrit): A being who, having developed the awakening mind, devotes his or her life to the task of achieving buddhahood for the sake of all sentient beings. One who has vowed to help all sentient beings rather than enjoy the state of enlightenment for himself or herself alone.

buddha nature: The potential that every sentient being has to become a buddha.

chang (Tibetan): Tibetan beer. Usually made from barley.

chuba (Tibetan): The traditional long dress worn by Tibetans. Men's chubas have long sleeves. Women's chubas are sleeveless and are often worn with a multicolored woven apron in front.

circumambulation: Purposeful, clockwise walks taken around a temple or stupa in order to accumulate spiritual merit or positive potential. This is a form of prayer performed, often daily, by almost all Tibetans.

dakini (Sanskrit): A female being somewhat similar to an angel. Some exist within cyclic existence, others are free from it. Dakinis also represent the feminine energy principle, associated with wisdom and intelligence, which may be either destructive or creative.

deities: A pantheon of archetypal deities or buddhas who may be envisioned in Buddhist meditation practices. They hold the potential to open one's imagination to the expanded powers of enlightened beings and provide role models for experiencing the qualities of enlightenment.

Dharma (Sanskrit): Teachings of the Buddha. When appearing with lowercase *d*, truth, religion, law; the basic elements or realities.

Green Tara: The deity, or goddess, of compassionate action and protection. She is usually depicted as sitting in a lotus-like position but with her right foot stretched out, ready to step with active compassion into the world. Her right hand is usually lying flat on her right knee, palm up, symbolizing giving. Her left hand is at the level of her heart and holds a blue lotus, which symbolizes power and purity.

Green Tara Mantra: A mantra of praise to Green Tara, often chanted in times of need for wisdom, compassion, or strength to overcome suffering, obstacles, or danger. The short form (OM TARE TUTTARE TURE SOHA) is commonly sung in cycles of three or twenty-one.

karma (Sanskrit): The doctrine that actions are followed by an inevitable result; there is action and reaction, or cause and effect; literally, action.

kata (Tibetan): Traditional long white blessing scarf. Customarily presented to people in greeting, to say good-bye, as a blessing, as an offering, or for good luck.

lama (Tibetan): Spiritual guide and teacher.

mala (Sanskrit): Tibetan prayer beads, similar to a rosary, usually on a string of 108 beads, used to count the number of prayers or mantras recited.

mandala (Sanskrit): The arrangement of deities or their emblems, usually in the form of a circle, emanating from a center expressing a pattern of energies; the universe of a buddha.

Manjusri (Sanskrit): The deity of wisdom, usually depicted with a sword to symbolize his power to cut through ignorance.

mantra (Sanskrit): A formula of Sanskrit words or syllables, expressing in sound the essence of a particular deity, quality, or power.

mo-mo (Tibetan): A dumpling, usually with a spicy meat mixture wrapped inside a dough shell.

nagas (Sanskrit): Subterranean beings or spirits similar to serpents or snakes.

nirvana (Sanskrit): Liberation from suffering and from the sorrowful cycle of death and rebirth, the goal of Buddhists everywhere.
rinpoche (Tibetan): A reincarnated or highly realized or educated lama.

rlung (Tibetan, pronounced *loong*): The standard translation for the Sanskrit word prana, rlung refers to the vital "winds" or energy of the body, ranging from the gross breath to the many subtle currents of energy that, flowing through an intricate network of channels, allows mental and physical functions to operate. It is similar to chi or ki in East Asian cultures.

stupa (Sanskrit): A dome-shaped monument containing relics or religious texts.

sutra (Sanskrit): A discourse preached by the Buddha.

tanka (Tibetan): A traditional, stylized religious painting, usually depicting deities and their lives. Also spelled *thanka*.

tantra (Sanskrit): A treatise containing the esoteric teachings of a particular spiritual practice, which deals with the transmutation of energy; also the method itself. The method leads to a state of union through the balance and synthesis of opposites. It involves the transformation of disturbing emotions into beneficial intuition and wisdom.

thugpa (Tibetan): Soup.

tsampa (Tibetan): A flour made by grinding popped barley grains. Also spelled *tsamba*.

vajra (Sanskrit): A tantric ritual object, consisting of a spherical center from which radiate two sets of curved spokes, generally five or nine in number. Meaning both "thunderbolt" and "diamond," it symbolizes all of their qualities: power, indestructibility, purity, and supremacy.

winds : The same as *rlung*.

yoga (Sanskrit): A psychophysical method of spiritual development, concerned with the direction of energy and consciousness.

yogi (Sanskrit): A meditator; a being who has developed calm abiding and special insight.

Bibliography

Alport, Catherine. "Crossing Cultures with Women." *Women of Power* (Summer, 1987).

The Ambrosia Heart Tantra: The Secret Oral Teaching on the Eight Branches of the Science of Healing, vol. 1. Annotated by Dr. Yeshe Dhonden. Translated by Jhampa Kelsang. Dharamsala, India: Library of Tibetan Works and Archives, 1977.

Avedon, John F. *In Exile From the Land of Snows*. New York: Knopf, 1984.

Beyer, Stephan. *The Cult of Tara: Magic and Ritual in Tibet*. Berkeley: University of California Press, 1978.

Chophel Kharitsang, Norbu. *Folk Culture of Tibet*. New Delhi, India: Library of Tibetan Works and Archives, 1983.

———. *Folk Tales of Tibet*. New Delhi, India: Library of Tibetan Works and Archives, 1984.

———. "Tibetan Superstitions Regarding Childbirth." *Tibetan Medicine*, series no. 7. New Delhi, India: Library of Tibetan Works and Archives, 1984.

Clifford, Terry. *Tibetan Buddhist Medicine and Psychiatry*. Maine: Samuel Weiser, 1984.

The Dalai Lama (Fourteenth). *Freedom in Exile*. New York: HarperCollins, 1990.

———. *The Kalachakra Tantra*. Translated and edited by Jeffrey Hopkins. London: Wisdom Publications, 1985.

———. *My Land and My People*. New York: McGraw-Hill, 1962.

The Dalai Lama and Galen Rowell. *My Tibet*. Berkeley: University of California Press, 1990.

David-Neel, Alexandra. *Magic and Mystery in Tibet*. New York: Dover, 1971.

Dhargyey, Geshe Ngawang. *Tibetan Tradition of Mental Development*. New Delhi, India: Library of Tibetan Works and Archives, 1974.

Dhonden, Dr. Yeshe. *Health Through Balance*. Translated and edited by Jeffrey Hopkins. Ithaca, New York: Snow Lion, 1986.

———. "Childbirth in Tibetan Medicine." *Tibetan Medicine*, series no. 1. Dharamsala, India: Library of Tibetan Works and Archives, 1980.

———. "Embryology in Tibetan Medicine." *Tibetan Medicine*, no. 1. Dharamsala, India: Library of Tibetan Works and Archives, 1980.

Dolma, Dr. Lobsang Khangkar. *Lectures on Tibetan Medicine*. New Delhi, India: Library of Tibetan Works and Archives, 1986.

Dorris, Michael. *The Broken Cord*. New York: Harper & Row, 1989.

Dunham, Carroll, Ian Baker, and Thomas Kelly. *Tibet: Reflections from the Wheel of Life*. New York: Abbeville Press, 1993.

Fremantle, Francesca, and Chögyam Trungpa, trans. with commentary. *The Tibetan Book of the Dead*. Boston: Shambhala, 1987.

Geshe Rabten and Geshe Dhargyey. *Advice from a Spiritual Friend: Buddhist Thought Transformation*. Boston: Wisdom Publications, 1996.

Goldstein, Melvyn C., and Cynthia M. Beall. *Nomads of Western Tibet*. Berkeley: University of California Press, 1990.

Illustrated Principles and Practices of Tibetan Medicine. Translated title of a bound replica of the traditional eleventh-century Tibetan text and accompanying illustrations used in studies of Tibetan medicine. Printed in Tibetan and Chinese only.

International Campaign for Tibet. *The International Tibet Resource Directory 1995*. 2d ed. Washington, D.C., 1995.

Kelly, Petra, Gert Bastian, and Pat Aiello, eds. *The Anguish of Tibet*. Berkeley: Parallax Press, 1991.

Lati Rinbochay and Jeffrey Hopkins. *Death, Intermediate State and Rebirth*. Ithaca, New York: Snow Lion, 1979.

MacKenzie, Vicki. *Reincarnation: The Boy Lama*. Boston: Wisdom Publications, 1996.

Maiden, Anne Hubbell. *Options for Healthy Birth*. Sausalito, Calif.: Marina Institute for Culture and Ecology, 1993.

Norbu, Namkhai. *On Birth and Life*. Translated by Enrico Dell'Angelo and Barry Simmons. Venice, Italy: Tipografia Commerciale Venezia, 1983.

Odent, Michel. *Primal Health*. London: Century Hutchinson, 1986.

Rapgay, Dr. Lobsang. *Tibetan Medicine: A Holistic Approach to Better Health*. Dharamsala, India: Tibetan Medical Sciences Series, 1985.

———. "Mind-Made Health: A Tibetan Perspective." *Mind and Mental Health in Tibetan Medicine*. New York: Potala Publications, 1988.

Sangay, Thubten. "Tibetan Rituals of Childbirth and Childcare." Translated by Gavin Kilty. *Tibetan Medicine*, series no. 7. New Delhi, India: Library of Tibetan Works and Archives, 1983.

———. *Tibetan Birth Ceremonies*. Dharamsala, India: Library of Tibetan Works and Archives, 1975.

Sakya, Jamyang, and Julie Emery. *Princess in the Land of Snows*. Boston: Shambhala, 1990.

Smith, Warren. *Tibetan Nation*. Colorado: Westview Press, 1996.

Sogyal Rinpoche. *The Tibetan Book of Living and Dying*. San Francisco: Harper, 1992.

Taring, Rinchen Dolma. *Daughter of Tibet*. London: Wisdom Publications, 1986.

Thurman, Robert A.F. *The Tibetan Book of the Dead*. New York: Bantam Books, 1994.

Unsigned news note. "Zong Rinpoche's Incarnation Discovered." *Tibetan Review* (June, 1990)

Index

About Wisdom Publications

Wisdom Publications, a not-for-profit publisher, is dedicated to making available authentic Buddhist works for the benefit of all. We publish books on Buddhism, Tibet, and related East-West themes along with translations of the sutras and tantras, commentaries and teachings of past and contemporary Buddhist masters, and original works by the world's leading Buddhist scholars. We publish our titles with the appreciation of Buddhism as a living philosophy and with the special commitment to preserve and transmit important works from all the major Buddhist traditions.

If you would like more information or a copy of our mail-order catalogue, please contact us at:

WISDOM PUBLICATIONS
199 Elm Street
Somerville, Massachusetts 02144-3195 USA
Telephone: (617) 776-7416
Fax: (617) 776-7841
E-mail: info@wisdompubs.org
Web Site: http://www.wisdompubs.org

The Wisdom Trust

As a not-for-profit publisher, Wisdom Publications is dedicated to the publication of fine Dharma books for the benefit of all sentient beings and dependent upon the kindness and generosity of sponsors in order to do so. If you would like to make a donation to Wisdom, please contact our office.

Thank you.

Wisdom Publications is a non-profit, charitable 501(c)(3) organization and a part of the Foundation for the Preservation of the Mahayana Tradition (FPMT).